Public Relations: A Primer for Business Executives

ORLY,

THanks for ALL Your
HELP AS PastCHAIR. And Contribution To Dept.
Have A GREAT 2009 !

Bob Petrausch

Public Relations: A Primer for Business Executives

Donald Grunewald (DBA, Harvard) Iona College,
Giri Dua (DBA-CSM-IGS), TASMAC, and Robert J.
Petrausch (Ed.D., Columbia) Iona College

iUniverse, Inc.
New York   Bloomington

Public Relations: A Primer for Business Executives

iUniverse books may be ordered through booksellers or by contacting:

iUniverse
1663 Liberty Drive
Bloomington, IN 47403
www.iuniverse.com
1-800-Authors (1-800-288-4677)

ISBN: 978-1-4401-0165-6 (pbk)
ISBN: 978-1-4401-0166-3 (ebk)
ISBN: 978-1-4401-0167-0 (cloth)

Library of Congress Control Number: 2008939978

Printed in the United States of America

iUniverse rev. date: 11/17/08

PUBLIC RELATIONS: A Primer for Business Executives

DONALD GRUNEWALD, DBA

Iona College
New Rochelle, New York, USA

GIRI DUA, DBA

Training & Advanced Studies in Management
and Communications Ltd.
Pune, India

ROBERT J. PETRAUSCH, EdD

Iona College
New Rochelle, New York, USA

Contents

Chapter 1

Development of Public Relations

IN THE BEGINNING: WORDS AND SYMBOLS

The practice of public relations, it has been claimed, is as old as human history. In this sense, public relations was seen in action when cavemen wanted their clans to join in a hunt or migrate to another area. Indeed, some of the basic elements of public relations, like the effort to communicate, to persuade, and to strike harmony among conflicting interests, have been practiced sporadically since the dawn of civilization. The term, however, is of comparatively recent origin. As a concept, it goes back to ancient times, but as a profession, it is a recent phenomenon.

The factors responsible for its growth and development are many and complex. Every society, every craft, owes a distinct debt to the past. How public relations evolved over the years to meet the changing requirement of the society gives us an insight into the many dimensions of a fascinating profession. The study of the historical context of public relations, therefore, is an essential part of today's growing professionalism.

The origin of public relations has been traced to the earliest recorded history. An ancient clay tablet, found in Iraq, told Sumerian farmers how to grow better crops over 4,000 years ago. Its functions were similar to today's public relations bulletins issued by agriculture departments. In ancient India, rulers often employed a surveillance team to feel the pulse of the people. In the Ramayana, there is a character called Bhadro who used to report to Rama about popular feelings. The Arabian Tales relates how the celebrated Sultan Haroon-Al-Rashid used to wander about every night in disguise to find out what the people really felt about his administration.

In ancient times, enlightened kings had what was called the "Bell of Justice." Ringing of the bell led to a personal hearing by the king, and anyone who was aggrieved by the failure of the administrative machinery could seek personal intervention by the king. The story of a cow ringing the bell to seek justice against the prince, who ran over her calf when riding his chariot, is told to illustrate aptly a system that was in vogue in those days.

In ancient Greece, the use of poetry to influence public opinion became so widespread that Plato advocated prohibition of all poetry — except when written for the state. Alexander the Great, it is known, employed people to publicize tales of his power and his sense of justice. The value and importance of public opinion in ancient Rome can be seen from the aphorism, "*Vox populi, vox Dei*" (the voice of the people is the voice of God). When Julius Caesar wrote his *Commentaries,* he was not merely writing a report; he was also trying to convince the Roman citizen that he was a great leader. Matthew, Mark, Luke, and John, apostles all, were public relations experts with their gospels for the propagation of Christianity. The politics of Machiavelli recognized the potential power of public opinion.

Guilds in medieval Europe were the first organized business groups. They spoke for business as a unit. They invented hallmarks to emphasize quality and reputation. Magna Carta (1215 AD) and the Peasants' Revolt (1381 AD) are perhaps some of the early manifestations of the people's power in England. Lord Chancellors acted as "keepers of the king's conscience" and in that capacity, acted as mediators between the government and the nobility, church, tradesmen, and craftsmen.

During the Middle Ages, roving minstrels spread messages from castle to castle and from town to town in an informal way. In the eleventh century, Pope Urban II persuaded thousands of people, including powerful monarchs, to join the Crusades against the Turks. But it was only with Gutenberg's invention of printing (1456 AD) that information was democratized. Common people became slowly aware of the value of their collective opinion.

Yet, this historical background has the relationship to modern public relations in the same way as the practice of medieval alchemy has to modern chemistry. These early campaigns were all aimed at presenting an image or influencing public opinion, and those goals continue to remain.

A movement can crystallize only when the socio-economic forces and the objective condition for its emergence are sufficiently powerful to call for a change. Public relations, too, is a typical product of the momentous socio-economic upheaval that swept almost all countries in the course of the 20th century, a time when humanity progressed from horse-driven carriage to space shuttle. The factors that led to its origin and development are many and complex.

Rapid industrialization gave rise to a corporate structure that created the need to shape a clear message in order to humanize industry, and as an inevitable corollary, followed urbanization — the concentration of masses of people in cities. Government, business, and all public institutions felt the need to communicate with this mass audience. In a desperate bid to live up to the expectations of a fast-growing middle class, the inevitable realization followed that private interest must coincide with public good.

Growth of mass media called for special expertise to understand what avenues of communication were available and how best and most quickly they could be utilized to reach the people. In such a situation, public relations emerged as a management tool to mediate with the many publics to which modern society gives a voice.

Public relations in the modern era was first practiced in America only because at the beginning of the 20th century, the socio-economic conditions that could pave the way for public relations emerged in the United States. But with rapid industrialization, growth of democracy, and emergence of public opinion, the movement soon spread to other countries.

MASS PRODUCTION ERA

In the early days of the mass production era, business tycoons betrayed an ugly lack of human consideration. They looked upon society as a private hunting ground for business exploitation. Vast technological progress was accomplished with little or no organized thought for the public interest involved. Businesspeople often cared more about profits than about health and safety and saw no need to justify their actions. Their contemptuous attitude is best summed up by the sneering remark of the railroad tycoon Colonel William Vanderbilt. Asked about the possible public reaction over the withdrawal of a service, he is reported to have exploded into a notorious exclamation that has since passed into public relations history: "The public? Why, sir, the public be damned."It also accurately described the attitude of business leaders in many countries. It was in those days that the cleavage between business and the public started growing. As a reaction to these robber barons, as they were often called, rose a group of authors and journalists who threatened to unveil their shady practices. Their writings, calculated to rouse people, gave a strident call for change. This led to a wave of sentiment for legislative reforms. Though unorganized, they represented the expression of a new social awakening. They strongly denounced the excesses of business and the timidity of the government.

Industrialists were frightened. They were made to see that industry had to take the public into account or else find their survival in jeopardy. They felt the dire need to set aside their veil of secrecy and speak out in self-defense. But unaccustomed to the ways of mutual understanding, they first turned to advertising and lawyers. Some sought to silence the critics in the press through the carrot and stick of advertisement, agreeing to insert one in the friendly press and threatening to withdraw it from the critical section. Many carried out advertising campaigns to restore public confidence in big business. It did not work. Some turned to press agents to refurbish their reputations. Most of these firms operated in secrecy and did not realize the two-way nature of communication. These hired people painted over the real problems and presented their clients in the best possible light.

Business was concerned almost exclusively with favorable publicity, no matter whether its action or politics merited public approval. People soon saw through the approach. Friction continued to grow and the chasm seemed wider than ever.

Laws were passed to limit the excesses of business, particularly in the United States. Workers organized into unions. Business was in trouble. The glaring discrepancies between the whitewashing effort of business and the all too visible inequities was an early example of a credibility gap.

Failure of their nationwide publicity efforts made business executives review the soundness of their steps. Out of the desperate need to earn respectability and the confidence of society, came the first manifestation of public relations as an organized part of business planning and thinking.

Interactive relationship

Into this scenario stepped Ivy Ledbetter Lee, a journalist. He was hired by the coal mine operators in 1906 to plead their case when workers went out on strike. Lee had enormous respect for the wisdom of the people. His contention was that the people should be honestly informed of the good news as well as the bad. It was his conviction that if the people were given the facts, they would make correct judgments.

In a revolutionary approach for his time, Lee suggested an interactive relationship between management and the workers. Lee advised the coal mine operators to inform the people of their policies and action rather than evade questioning. "The public," Lee insisted, "was no longer to be ignored, in the manner of the press agents." He developed a new policy of "the public be informed" to replace the hitherto practiced one of "the public be damned."

Lee put this new approach to work in the coal strike. On behalf of the company, he adopted a policy of open communication, helping journalists to cover the event in every possible way.

While Lee was working for the Pennsylvania Railroad, there was a major accident and a number of lives were lost. To avoid embarrassment, the authorities decided to hush it up. Lee, however, firmly pointed out that a wreck could not be hidden and the people were sure to find out the truth. He succeeded in persuading the railroad to run special trains for the press to the accident spot. He also organized compensation for the families of those killed and hospitalization of the injured. He made the company undertake a system-wide survey so that similar accidents might not occur again. The press widely appreciated the measures taken following the accident. They liked particularly the honesty and openness that characterized the company's dealings — in sharp contrast to the prevalent practice of hide and hoodwink.

Lee always insisted that he was serving not only the interests of the industry, but also the interests of the people. He made some basic contributions to the growth of public relations. One was that he discovered the importance of humanizing business. He was the first to voice the concept of corporate social responsibility for business. The other was that he declined to accept any assignment unless he was convinced he had the active support and personal participation of the top management.

The First World War further underscored the value of public relations as a tool to enter into a dialog with the people. U.S. President Woodrow Wilson set up the Committee of Public Information with George Creel, a journalist, as chairman. The Creel Committee exhibited the power of organized public relations to enlist people's support for a cause. The war of words, it was seen, was no less a factor than the war of shells in determining the eventual outcome. Edward Bernays, a young member of the Creel Committee, later remarked: "This was the first time in history that information was used as a weapon of war."

Bernays, a nephew of Sigmund Freud, was the first to apply Freudian and modern psychological perspectives to public relations. He also wrote the first book on public relations, *Crystallizing Public Opinion*, in 1923. Bernays provided public relations with a strong academic base, a scientific approach, and a professional respectability. He also introduced the first course in public relations at New York University in 1923. Bernays consolidated what Lee had begun.

The Great Depression in the early thirties in the United States brought a new challenge as well as an opportunity for the fledgling profession. Wealth became suspect during the great economic crisis. Business was cast as a villain. Simultaneously, in a grave financial situation, public relations was one of the first services to be curtailed. But at the same time, business began to realize slowly that to ensure its survival in an increasingly hostile atmosphere, it was not enough to sell its products, it had also to sell itself. It also marked the beginning of a new era of social responsibilities of business. Industry began to realize that publicity intended merely to whitewash its sins would no longer be acceptable. A change in the attitude of the public toward business could be brought about only if business reformed itself.

In a speech before the Association of National Advertisers, the president of a large U.S. company enunciated this new philosophy as an essential tool for survival in the changed milieu: "Too many manufacturers neglect their corporate health and then scream for the public relations herb doctors. Any public relations worthy of its name must start with the business itself. Unless the business is so organized and so administered that it can meet at every point the test of good citizenship and of usefulness to the community, no amount of public relations will avail."

The outbreak of World War II demonstrated once again the necessity of using public relations in marshaling public opinion. The Office of War Information (OWI), set up by the U.S. government, encouraged extensive application of public relations in the armed forces, in industry, and in allied fields. The growth of academic courses in public relations in the universities throughout the United States, along with the job opportunities, brought public relations to a point of high professional excellence. Boston University started a program in public relations in 1947.

The first signs of organized public relations in the United Kingdom were visible in 1911 through the efforts of the Insurance Commission to explain the National Insurance Act. World War I also saw the rapid growth of official publicity in Britain and its colonies. The Ministry of Information carried on propagation of the British policies and lent active support to war efforts. Press relations was also growing in importance. The post of Press Secretary to the King was created in 1918 and a chief press liaison officer was appointed in the prime minister's office. During World War II, the Ministry of Information was revived to aid the war effort. The Institution of Public Relations, set up in 1948, played a significant role in the development of the profession. It is interesting to observe that while public relations in the United States grew in stature predominantly in the business and industrial spheres, the main impetus in Britain for its development came primarily from the government.

It was generally assumed that business would return to tough competitive selling after the War and that public relations programs would suffer a decline. But business had discovered the power and, inferentially, the menace of public opinion. This meant assuming greater responsibility for the public welfare in order to create understanding with the society.

New aspirations

Meanwhile, emergence of many new and democratic countries, which broke off the imperialist domination in the post-war years, lent an altogether new dimension to the necessity and practice of public relations. The growth of a new society in all these countries comprising people with yearnings for progress and better lives made the role of public relations increasingly important as a mediator, interpreter, and communicator. The growing diversity of people and their varied interests required greater skill in counseling the management to formulate an appropriate message along with the selection of suitable channels to reach them.

The increasing incidents of change, conflict, and confrontation also created the necessity for a group of professional people who understood people's attitudes and aspirations. From its first uncertain steps in the United States in the early part of this century, public relations grew into a major societal force in more than a hundred countries. Practice of public relations at the international level had experienced accelerated growth as much as national public relations because of multiplying foreign markets and the complexity of global politics with the collapse of the Soviet Union and the end of the Cold War.

CHAPTER 2

Basic Concepts of Public Relations

The nature and scope of public relations is difficult to categorize. People tend to supply their own meanings to the term, interpreting its functions according to their own experiences or biases. The title itself is used indiscriminately, the duties encompassed by the practice are expanding, and the many uninformed criticisms often obscure the true role of public relations.

Although many observers would deny the status of a "profession" to public relations, claiming it doesn't meet the usual professional requirements of a specific body of knowledge, a unified set of standards, and an appropriate testing procedure, there are those who would contend that PR, properly practiced, is a profession demanding as many skills and insights as most other professions. Increasing academic attention to public relations courses and degrees, the existence of a code of conduct, and the promotion of accreditation procedures seem, to these adherents, to meet professional qualifications. They point out that the practice can have a positive effect on society by presenting a deeper view of various social entities. Public relations campaigns may rebut dissidents, squelch harmful rumors, promote decent health habits, argue for safety, or abet progressive political notions. It can be rewarding to the practitioner, essential to the manager, and efficient for the consumer.

TOWARD A DEFINITION

Public relations can mean a course of action, a state of acceptance or non-acceptance, or it can describe an entire profession. It also seems to expand or contract with organizations, depending on whether others seek to use the PR budget for their projects — which are invariably defined as "excellent public relations" — or whether they want to protect their own domain, in which case "public relations" is given its narrowest scope.

Given these difficulties, various organizations and publications offer their definitions, which, although perhaps incomplete, serve as guides to the practice.

The *American Heritage Dictionary* defines public relations as "the activities taken by an organization to promote a favorable relationship with the public."

Purists would have all sorts of quarrels with that definition. It seems to ignore the research and planning functions, the evaluation aspects, and the management posture that supports these activities.

Various public relations groups and each new textbook assembles individual definitions. These get longer and longer. Among the shorter ones are these:

> . . . *good performance publicly appreciated because adequately communicated. (Fortune)*

> . . . *the management function designed to increase profits, or the equivalent, directly or indirectly, by earning public goodwill through the adoption and continuing communication to the public of policies and procedures acceptable or beneficial to all concerned. (PR Reporter)*

Management function

This stresses the fact that the public relations function within a firm operates at the highest level, helping to formulate and implement organizational goals and advising executives on strategies to be employed to reach such goals. This is not a sales responsibility or an advertising responsibility, not even strictly a promotional responsibility; it is part of management's consideration and conduct.

Public interest

These words remind practitioners that immediate and long-range considerations must be given to any action that affects the public. Furthermore, the professional knows that public relations consists not of making something wrong seem right, but of correcting the flaw and then publicizing the results.

Evaluation

Before any plans are approved or enacted, a research phase occurs — the gathering of information to help make any later decisions as intelligently as possible. This evaluation continues through the campaign and after the campaign.

Planning

A person or an organization may accidentally garner favorable publicity. An aspiring politician might rescue a drowning child and consequently reap favorable publicity. Or a conveniently located company could shelter motorists during a sudden snowstorm and earn praise for its hospitality. Although these events constitute good public relations in the generic sense, they are not public relations in the professional sense because they are accidental. Planning remains the operative word.

Acceptance

Normally, the goal of public relations efforts is acceptance by special publics or the general public. This could mean an opinion change or opinion development or, with regard to your friends, opinion retention. The end result may be purchase of a product, contribution of funds, support of a candidate or issue, or even a general mood of approval.

Public

Any group of people interested in an issue at any one time might constitute a public, as might any segment of society you seek to interest. Public relations campaigns, when they are most effective and efficient, concentrate on a set of publics rather than attempting to reach everyone.

Also within every examination of public relations is the formula that practitioners must teach to their students: **R.A.C.E.**

"**R**" stands for *research*, "**A**" stands for *action*, "**C**" for *communication*, and "**E**" for *evaluation*. Some might argue for expanding that acronym to embrace planning, but it's a handy recipe to remember when reviewing any problem or devising any campaign. Students tackling case problems also find the short checklist invaluable.

Even within these broad limits, some professionals debate the meaning and priority of certain definitive terms. One chief executive officer feels that counseling and communication, as important as they are, should take a back seat to the conciliatory aspect of public relations, pointing out that practitioners are uniquely qualified, because of their sensitivity and experience, to keep the internal and external company environment functioning smoothly. Edward L. Bernays wants to expunge the word *image* from the public relations lexicon, arguing that *image* suggests "illusion," whereas public relations concerns itself with reality.

WHAT ABOUT ADVERTISING AND PUBLICITY?

Although it isn't possible to draw a firm distinction between advertising and public relations in specific instances, the major difference is that advertising is a marketing function and public relations is a management function. The former relates to the activities required to sell an organization's products or services and is reflective of market conditions and directed by marketing strategists; the latter attempts to "sell" the organization itself and initiates management decisions to achieve that goal. It's not a neat division, since there is considerable overlapping. PR can be used to sell products, and advertising may be employed for public relations purposes. Both use persuasive techniques and both have recourse to mass media. Normally, advertising has more control over time and space since it pays for both, whereas public relations has to earn "free" coverage in newspapers, radio, and television and cannot guarantee such placement. But PR does control some media items, like brochures, annual reports, films, and other promotional tools. Neither is public relations "free," since there are salaries to pay, travel, equipment, and other operating expenses.

In practice, most persons could pick out an ad and recognize it for what it is, leaving the majority of other promotional efforts in the PR arena. There is also much current discussion over the wisdom of merging the services of ad agencies and public relations agencies. Larger advertising firms already have their PR divisions, but many of them seek added strength by acquiring very successful public relations agencies. One reason for such mergers is to provide a top-flight full-service capability; another is to prevent the potential loss of advertising clients who might be weaned away when they require certain PR expertise. The debate over such mergers centers on the relative profitability of advertising versus public relations (advertising is generally more profitable) and the tensions that could develop among people coming from different backgrounds.

Publicity, which is often confused with public relations, is really just a tool of the larger PR concept. Publicity involves the placement of stories in the mass media and is an important element in the public relations process. However, it is possible to have wide, even favorable, publicity and still not have good public relations. The reported activities of an institution, for example, could be considered interesting, entertaining, newsworthy. Later, the public exposed to these stories may be asked to approve a zoning change affecting the institution or a bond issue required for expansion. Their image of the organization, influenced by the news stories, could fail to support this serious request because they view the publicity as essentially trivial.

Then, too, any firm could choose or not choose to have publicity, to a considerable degree. Unless some major event occurred, like a fire or a robbery, chances are the overworked media would not be hurrying to this company to dig out news stories.

With public relations, there is no such choice. You have it — good, bad, or indifferent. As coaches say about the forward pass, "Only three things can happen, and two of them are bad." Ditto for public relations. The public may think well of you, think ill of you, or be indifferent or ignorant.

Publicity also suffers by being one-way communication, whereas public relations strives to generate dialog and feedback. It is a more complex, comprehensive discipline.

WHO NEEDS PUBLIC RELATIONS?

Few organizations argue against the wisdom of including public relations in their plans. It wasn't always this way. Some firms used to believe they could be trusted to ultimately realize the right stance in any given situation. Today, even the smallest firms try to present some sort of PR program.

Why?

Simply because public relations works. Even when a company is performing well, the public needs to be told about it. And when an organization has problems, the PR function has proved its ability to provide solutions or, at the very least, to ensure that the client firm is able to tell its version of the debate.

With the increase in corporate, even conglomerate, structure, interpersonal relations are bound to suffer. It's a long way from the person at the desk to the person at the machine, or from the nurse in the ward to the chief of staff. Communication gaps are vast, and the human touch is difficult to simulate. Public relations programs can help shorten the distance between executive and subordinate.

Externally, relationships are even more complicated. The average citizen understands less and less about government, education, space, economics, and dozens of other complex subjects. And this confusion has occurred at a time when we boast the most sophisticated and far-reaching communications systems in history. The public relations professional seeks to cut through to the public's consciousness, providing it with a message that will be understood and retained.

When Apple Computer introduced its products, one of the firm's concerns was the reluctance of adults to learn this new skill. Giving the units friendly names, utilizing a simple logo, presenting the executives as bright young innovators — all these things were tied into the ad campaign, which positioned the Apple computers as easy to operate and fun to own, making them accessible to both young and old.

Communicators like Jack Welch, former GE chairman, president, and CEO, succeed because they seem to be able to bring business problems and decisions within reach of the average viewer or reader. A year's activities, its triumphs and failures, its profits and losses, all have to be summarized within a few pages of an annual report.

Public relations may not show up on the "bottom line" of a corporate report, as a lawsuit, tax lien, or product breakthrough might, but it's just as real and exercises similar influence on profitability. Modern managers know this. They understand that a poorly timed news story could destroy public confidence and bring down the market value of their stock. They know that an unsettled grievance may lead to a strike and subsequent loss of revenue. In a society as fragmented as ours, no company or organization can afford to ignore public relations.

However, public relations can't accomplish miracles — and it shouldn't promise any. Exaggerating one's ability to place stories in the media can have damaging results for the whole profession; so can the inclusion of celebrities as instant PR persons, and the ineptness of certain members of the vocation. Destructive, too, is the failure of management to fully trust and utilize the PR function. Practitioners often complain that the person hired to handle public relations is saddled with all sorts of entry-level communications tasks that are important in themselves, but is given no real management role.

All too often, public relations is viewed as "firefighting" instead of fire prevention. There are countless cases where good day-to-day public relations could have prevented the need for often unsuccessful damage control efforts. It often takes a crisis to wake up management to the benefits of communicating with the public on a major scale.

Whether the aim is to improve the sales curve or alter public policy, to raise funds or to raise issues, PR is a 21ˢᵗ century force and phenomenon.

CHAPTER 3

No intelligent person would begin a journey without a map. In fact, the seasoned traveler wants to know climate conditions, tips on appropriate clothing, the rate of exchange for money, the political situation, perhaps even some research would be useful — basic perhaps, but still valuable.

Any public relations decision or program merits the same sort of initial scrutiny. Public relations relies on the information-gathering process. It requires facts, not intuition or assumptions. You must have these facts at hand or know where to get them. To proceed without such data is unprofessional and dangerous.

Despite that truism, public relations has not been exemplary in its use of research. Frequently, clients or marketing departments supply the research data and practitioners work from it.

There is also a shortage of research materials in the field of public relations, compared, for example, with marketing, politics, and other areas. Practitioners need more information on behavior, on organizational theory, and on legal matters. Leaders in the public relations arena seem aware of this and, in the past several years, steps have been instituted to correct it. A new journal, *Public Relations Research and Education*, was launched in 1984 by the PR division of the Association for Education in Journalism and Mass Communication, and the PRSA's Foundation for Public Relations Research and Education sponsors competitions for the most significant research efforts relating to the profession. In judging Silver Anvil (the top PRSA awards) winners, PRSA committees also say more weight will be given to research-backed entries than those lacking proof of planning or effectiveness.

VALUE OF RESEARCH

The prediction of election results, the assessment of television viewer preferences, and the solicitation of opinion on new products are familiar forms of research, but the list of uses in public relations is extensive.

Basically, PR research is used to verify, clarify, or identify:

▶ Assumptions about conditions affecting a company or its publics may need to be verified by some form of research. A public relations officer may think that the company publication is not being read very frequently or thoroughly; a survey could produce a factual basis to support or contradict this hunch.

▶ Occasionally, conflicting reports make decisions more difficult, information may be incomplete, or the reasons for beliefs or behavior may be clouded. One needs to clarify the data. What do respondents mean when they say "favor stricter penalties for drunk drivers?" Why are employees indifferent to a proposed major medical benefit package?

Research can also identify problem areas or opportunities, allowing administrators to plan more effectively. A decline in enrollment is a signal to educators preparing a budget. A general ignorance about the consumer advantages inherent in a certain new law will convince a federal agency that more communication is required.

Editors of business publications periodically survey readership, trying to discover if they are really doing their job. Questions asked might include the following:

▶ What do you like or dislike in the publication?

▶ What would you like to see more of? less of?

▶ How much of the publication do you read?

▶ How much time do you spend reading the publication?

▶ What other members of your family read the publication?

▶ Do you discuss with others the stories you read?

You could also ask readers to categorize the style, to comment on the paper stock used, to advise on frequency of mailing, even to suggest a new publication title.

There are formal and informal methods for gathering information. The formal methods may be more statistically reliable, but the informal have real value and, in some instances, may even be preferred. The internet has become a powerful research tool for public relations executives in the new digital age.

PUBLIC RELATIONS PLANNING AND CREATIVITY

Once the public relations practitioner has assembled the raw data — the product of research — and has considered the modifications dictated by the current environment, he or she is ready to enter the planning stage.

Planning is nothing more than the determination of goals for an organization and the outlining of means to achieve these goals. Fundraisers have a slogan: *Plan your work, then work your plan.* This is sound advice. No one would lay carpeting or cut out a garment without a pattern. And a contractor doesn't pour a foundation without studying the architect's blueprint. If the pattern and the planning are accurate, the work goes smoothly; if not, the project flounders.

Planning encompasses every phase of a business or organization, and it involves personnel at every level. Public relations professionals not only employ planning in their work, but must also be cognizant of the planning of others that affects their function.

Planning may be possible, preventive, or remedial. A PR person may want to originate a salutary project, or may anticipate a negative situation and take measures to prevent it, or may have to correct an already harmful condition.

A cable TV company ran a full-page advertisement in the Sunday paper promoting its security service. The response was good, but when the interested customers phoned the number given in the ad, they heard a recording — the cable company was closed on Sunday. Eighty percent of the callers hung up without giving their names.

Conversely, New College, Oxford, founded in the late sixteenth century in England, discovered a few years ago that the oak beams in its great dining hall were being eroded by beetles, a fate common to oak beams everywhere. The disconsolate College Council, certain that no oak beams of that caliber were available today, summoned the College Forester, the person responsible for tending college lands. He said he was expecting their call and was able to reassure them. When the College was built, a grove of oak was also planted, in preparation for the day when beetles would ravage the original beams. Now 400 years old, these oaks were ready for "harvesting" as replacement beams. This plan had been passed down from Forester to Forester from the time of Queen Elizabeth I.

Planning affects the large picture and the small picture. Some economists are arguing against international government intervention in economic planning, as mass production becomes more flexible and supply and demand more imbalanced. At the same time, luncheon hosts are discussing the menu with a caterer and invitations with the printer.

STEPS IN PLANNING

Although each plan has its own unique features, the steps taken in planning are rather similar. They include:

▶ Gathering of data

▶ Analysis of data

▶ Identification of problem or opportunity

▶ Examination of past experience

▶ Examination of the experience of others

▶ Consideration of future developments

▶ Evaluation of alternatives

▶ Selection of the best alternative

▶ Weighting of positive and negative factors

▶ Implementation of a plan

▶ Monitoring of the plan

Gathering of data

All the information necessary to a thoughtful and thorough consideration of the subject should be assembled. Collecting such data may mean employing both formal and informal research methods. Many companies have their own research divisions that can produce such details and thus ensure more decisions. Planners must also know their own organizations well, understanding who they are and who they are not, what their strengths and weaknesses are, where they are going, and who their target audiences are.

Once derived, this research information should be organized into easily understood units so those participants in planning may have ready access to data they need.

Analysis of data

The facts are examined — realistically. This takes an open mind and more than a little skill. Each piece of evidence is sifted for meaning. Each element is examined for potential harm or help to the institution. Future developments are postulated, and relationships to organizational goals are studied.

Identification of problem or opportunity

After sufficient discussion, the problem or opportunity should emerge. The company may discern that it is falling behind the competition in certain sales areas. The public relations director may isolate a rumor that is destroying employee morale. A news bureau chief senses a publicity coup.

Whatever the focus becomes in this planning facet, every attempt should be made to produce a conclusion that is both specific and clear.

Examination of past experience

If history repeats itself, then so do problems. Faced with a difficulty, practitioners should review their own experience for similar situations and then check the records to determine root causes. Success or failure with related situations in the past may exhibit clues for future conduct.

Suppose a financial public relations adviser is proposing a breakfast meeting with all regional financial analysts. In checking all past records, he or she discovers that a similar breakfast held four years earlier was poorly attended, and there were complaints about the early hour. This should lead to the adviser's contacting a sample of analysts to see if this situation still exists. If it does, a change in time should be considered.

When one company reviewed its hiring practices with an eye toward attracting applicants with broader backgrounds, it examined its past record on bias in selecting interviewees, its testing routines, the entry level jobs it had offered successful candidates, recurring deficiencies it had noted in applicants, its integration of women and minorities into various departments, and its record of conformity with national norms.

Examination of the experience of others

Few topics in public relations are unique. Chances are that all PR problems have been experiences somewhere else and that all innovations have precedents.

Many associations maintain lending libraries of case histories. CASE (Council for the Advancement and Support of Education), for example, an amalgam of collegiate fundraisers, alumni officers, and public relations directors, keeps elaborate files on all sorts of subjects — from class picnics to multimedia recruiting tools. Other associations may incorporate case histories as part of their regular publications.

There will be others, who can be reached by phone, mail, email, or in person, whose counsel may save the practitioner from costly error. Those conducting an anniversary celebration for their company or organization would certainly want to review the printed or oral record of those who have managed a similar event; those assembling their initial PR plan would be aided by a look at an existing plan.

Consideration of future developments

Planners always consider the effect of the future on the programs being inaugurated. Although the future cannot be predicted with certainty, there are observable signs that may indicate caution or encourage optimism. This is where the knowledge of trends helps.

In reality, the long run is just a series of short runs and it's important we try to look beyond the short run to examine the long-run inputs of our plans and directions.

Evaluation of alternatives

Every problem has more than one solution. In planning sessions, alternatives are laid on the table for consideration. Most of these suggestions have positive and negative features. Frequently, they will compete with one another. Anything from the selection of a date to the introduction of a new product will have its list of choices. The greater the number of options one has, the greater the likelihood of a prudent, effective recommendation.

Selection of the best alternative

After the alternatives have been weighted, a decision must be made. Sometimes planners get bogged down in the process itself, convinced that the very act of planning is the end and not the means. This cannot be allowed to happen. Ultimately, some proposal must meet with acceptance and some method must be adopted.

Weighting of positive and negative factors

When a specific alternative has been embraced, there should be further discussion about the consequences of this choice.

➤ What harm could result?

▶ What publics might be adversely affected?

▶ What future difficulties might arise?

▶ Can we afford it?

If we allow an employee a discount on the automobiles we manufacture, will this action irritate the stockholders? If we institute a fringe benefit offering tuition-free scholarships to the children of employees, will we be able to handle the escalating college costs in the years ahead?

Implementation of plan

At an appropriate time, the plan is launched and its dictates are pursued until the goal is reached or until the planners are convinced the attempt is a failure. In the latter case, it is back to the drawing board and the process repeats itself.

During the implementation phase of any plan, cooperation and commitment are required. This suggests that key people should be involved early and their support won, and that all others should buy in as soon as the plan is operable. If important personnel drag their feet, if funding dries up, if too little time has been allotted, if significant publics have been ignored — these and others lapses could doom an otherwise satisfactory plan.

Monitoring of plan

As the plan is being implemented, the professional practitioner makes observations, obtains feedback from participants, and draws preliminary conclusions. If results look questionable, some adjustments may be required. If, on the other hand, the plan is working out better than expected, this may be the time to commit additional money and personnel to exploit the success. Conversely, if the implementation phase is faring badly, it may warrant cancellation. There is no sense in waiting until disaster strikes.

PUBLIC RELATIONS PLANNING

Just as with other divisions of a company or organization, public relations personnel have to compose, implement, and evaluate their own specific plan. As they do so, the overall goal of the employer or client must be considered, along with the possible effect on society.

When things are going fairly smoothly, public relations practitioners are often reluctant to examine their programming, even though it may be operating under guidelines fashioned earlier, when the company was substantially different.

Writing in *Public Relations Journal*, Elaine Goldman concludes, "It's amazing how many corporate communications departments are outdated, even in Fortune 500 companies." She poses a series of questions to help professionals determine whether or not the communications system needs overhauling.

▶ Have the corporate objectives been delineated in terms of such factors as your company's business, markets, capital needs, growth plans, industry, and, most significant, the vision of the chief executive officer?

▶ Is your company in a business that is becoming increasingly more affected by such external factors as government regulation, industry maturity, increased competition, changing structures of capital markets, new technologies, and public attitudes? Does your company need more representation in the capital of the country?

▶ If the chairperson is fairly new, how are his or her methods different from those of the previous chair? Does the chairperson want high visibility or prefer to function internally? How does the chairperson perceive visibility as a corporate tool? How does the chairperson perceive the role of communication in marketing?

▶ Have the capital market needs of the company changed? Does the company need to be better known to the financial community?

▶ Have the relationships between internal and external communication changed?

▶ Is the communication strategy for positioning the company supported by all divisions and in all published materials (including advertising)? Does the communication department structure support this concept?

▶ Do communication employees have strong skills?

▶ Have orientations changed? For example, has corporate presence become more important than marketing presence? Should investor relations have a higher profile? Is product exposure becoming more of a factor than institutional visibility?

▶ Should the company participate more in debates on issues that affect its business climate?

▶ Are departmental lines of reporting and responsibility responsive to the needs of the company?

▶ While these elements are being weighed, the PR person must also be considering what effect various publics, including competition, may have on the organization, be aware of what the media are saying about the company, and be up on new legislation that could alter the way the firm does business.

Like any other plan, the public relations plan starts with fact-gathering, pays attention to the publics involved, and to the competition, sets down realizable goals, delineates ways of reaching these goals, and builds in a system of evaluation. Wise planners also make sure they don't commit all their time to the new regimen. Some unforeseen circumstances are certain to crop up and will require immediate action, so the practitioner should have some contingency time to be used for emergencies. The planner must also keep things in balance, remembering all the tasks at hand and allotting appropriate amounts of time for each.

Communicators must persevere in their planning, even though they know that an organization's future plans may not always give public relations the billing it deserves.

Management has always been obliged to identify first with their marketing and profit responsibilities. The emphasis may vary, but not the priority.

Perhaps there is some consolation in the recognition that a company's plans rank first in terms of what employees read in their company's publications, scoring higher than personnel policies and job advancement. And there may be some adjunct psychic benefits.

Giving the public relations staff the opportunity to participate in management — to see its own thoughts help form program plans — can increase creativity, efficiency, and the overall effectiveness of the public relations function.

ELEMENTS OF A PLAN

Any plan involves six elements:

▶ The reasons for the plan

▶ The goals or objectives of the plan

▶ The current status of the organization vis-à-vis these objectives

▶ The methods of implementation to be used

▶ The target audiences

▶ The cost

Every plan should have a purpose, or reason for being. Manufacturers want to increase sales; promoters want to build attendance; politicians want to ensure elections. A hospital public relations director may want to correct a misinterpretation of hospital charges, or expand publicity coverage, or blunt the attack of an opposition group.

Goals and objectives will also vary. These are not interchangeable terms. Goals are usually described as the end result of a campaign (or a series of campaigns), whereas objectives constitute the things that must be done to reach these goals. A PR campaign for a new hybrid car would call for a strong media relations campaign for key stakeholders.

The current relationship of the organization to the goals and objectives must be determined. Perhaps only slight adjustments must be made because the institution is already close to its goal. This plan may be short and simple. If, on the other hand, the goals are far removed from present reality, considerable planning will be mandatory.

Actions to be taken or methods to be employed are spelled out. These are specific activities under each objective. Now that the planners have decided what they want to do and why, they must wrestle with "how."

Let us assume the need is to neutralize a group of neighborhood protestors who are blocking a proposed low-income housing for deprived citizens and the objective is to remove the roadblock of protest. Should the issue be forced through the courts? Should the objectors be invited to a public forum? Should literature be mailed to all dissidents? Should a media campaign be waged to discredit the motives of the neighborhood group? Should the poor be mobilized to hold a counter-protest? One or more of these alternatives may be selected, weighted, and implemented.

Also requiring consideration is the audience for communications. Who are the people who must be reached? Where are they located, and what is the most effective and efficient way to reach them? When is the best time to make contact?

Careful planners list all possible target audiences, perhaps breaking them into primary and secondary publics. No relevant group should be omitted. It is safer to err on the side of encompassing too broad a public segment than to take the chance of missing a vital group.

The trick, of course, is to personalize the approach to each group as much as possible. In a hospital, the physician might receive a different message than the nurse, and the nurse a different message than the trustee or patient. Faculty, students, and alumni would be treated in different ways since their interests and information vary. Military units would have unique communications for legislators, senior officers, junior officers, enlisted personnel, and hometown newspapers.

The more the PR practitioner knows about each group, the better the message he or she can design.

BUDGETING

Obviously, cost enters into nearly every plan. When you are examining the accepted plan for weaknesses, you must consider the budget requirements. Perhaps the most effective way to communicate with a specific audience is via prime time television — but can you afford it? The price of paper, printing, and postage may limit your direct mail appeal to a smaller segment of the populace than you initially intended. Although the dollar amounts may be important in themselves, even more important is the effectiveness of those dollars. Television, for example, may still be the best solution, even though it costs much more, because it reaches more of the people you want to reach at a lower per-unit cost. And today, a campaign may be conducted just using the internet.

Planners must know what things cost and cannot guess at prices. They must also be realistic and not let their desire for a solution cloud their reason.

Some plans start with a set budget figure and everything is tailored to fit. ("You have ten thousand to spend on this party and that's it.")

Others first outline things to be accomplished, then put dollar figures on them, and then request a commensurate budget.

Too much of the budgeting for public relations (and for advertising) is haphazard. Some figures are virtually pulled out of a hat. Others are extensions of a previous year's expenditures, or a match for a competitor's expenses, or the result of someone's reading that a certain percentage of profits should be allocated to advertising and promotion. There is no magic percentage that covers all situations. It is not five percent or 10 percent. It could be more or it could be less.

The sanest concept is to match the budget to the need. What will it take to do the job properly? An organization just starting up may need to commit a higher percentage of its profit than one with an established reputation. A firm with nationwide clients is going to find it more expensive to communicate than will a local company.

The budget for any activity is both a "goal" and a "control." You strive to stay within the amount originally determined, and you use this figure to decide on and monitor expenses. That's why careful attention should be given to this factor in the early stages of planning and why it also needs constant administration.

As with any other aspect of public relations, you first do your research, ascertaining what expenses are likely to be and what objectives will be realized. Then you approve or cut, communicating the budget figures to others and monitoring their use.

It's a smart practice to list all conceivable expenditures for any PR activity and to talk these over with others who might provide input. Make certain that you have included all possible expenditures and that you've left a cushion for emergencies. Regardless of the variations, good budgeting technique involves common sense, detailed analysis, experience, and administrative courage and ability.

No one can escape budgeting; this is obvious. Even when you plan a personal vacation, you include transportation, lodging, meals, fees for entertainment, and tips — perhaps, if you are a careful budgeter, even airport taxes, luggage transfers, refreshments, and gifts. Planning for a major public relations event is similar — only the items are different.

Priorities

One plan usually gives rise to another. If you are to accomplish this, you must do this. Some plans will have priority over others, and some activities must take precedence over others.

Public relations executives recognize that the key words in any PR program are *priority* and *discipline*:

> **Priority** *demands that your common sense recognize that any program must have a realistic, achievable goal. . . .* **Discipline** *means the guts to stick to the plan and the program and not be seduced by peripheral projects, the spontaneity of which is always more appealing than the drudgery of programmed commitments.*

> **Caution:** *The practitioner must weigh one assignment against another, and to orient the program to the objectives of the corporation. It is suggested to allocate time on a percentage basis, and the listing of priorities as primary, secondary, and optional:*

> *. . . you can't spend all of your time writing stories; you can't spend all of your time being available to the "drop-in" trade, visiting plant managers for internal goodwill purposes, or sitting in on interminable meetings.*

MAKING THE MOST OF YOUR TIME

There's a cottage industry devoted to helping people make better use of their time. Books abound on the subject, and periodic conferences promise to teach you *"How to get a thing done!"* In these sessions you learn how to say no, how to cope with interruptions, how to deal with superiors, how to avoid doing everything yourself, and how to recognize when you should let well enough alone.

Other experts counsel short vacations to refresh the mind, the setting of time limits on each working day, developing the ability to laugh at your mistakes, getting more mileage out of each thing you do, and learning what you must do, what you can defer, what you can delegate, and what you can forget.

"Work smarter, not harder," they advise.

DECISION MAKING

All the research and planning go for naught if the person who controls the implementation process can't make a decision — or won't make a decision. Some executives can't stand being wrong, or they fear reprisals, or they don't want to chance losing any friendships. They may appeal to higher authority, try to find a safe, standard solution, pass the buck to a subordinate, clutch wildly at an apparent solution, or do nothing and hope the problem will disappear.

The informed and confident executive, however, is not cowed by a challenge. Having diligently passed through the planning process, this executive selects and blesses one of the options. The ability and willingness to do this is a characteristic that sets good managers apart.

TYPES OF PLANNING

Short- and long-range plans

Short-range plans are intended to meet a somewhat immediate need, whereas long-range plans attempt to forecast future trends or state future goals. The latter may have a scope of five, 10, or more years.

Chief executives are likely to spend a high percentage of their planning time on long-range matters, whereas departmental supervisors or shop supervisors may concentrate more on plans for that day, week, or month.

Short-range planning takes less time to create and is specific. Long-range planning takes longer, is more general, and, because of the time lag, is more prone to error.

Every organization should have a long-range plan. This is the only way to exhibit corporate leadership, to integrate individuals and departmental effort, to act rather than react, and to enjoy the relative luxury of some deliberation time in periods of crisis.

From the public relations viewpoint, long-range planning prevents myriad headaches. Unless there is a plan, it is difficult to assess daily chores properly, or to measure results, or to document efficiently for a client or supervisor, or to convince a comptroller of the need for funds.

With proper planning, new programs can be boldly formulated instead of being timidly defended. Real needs can be demonstrated and a sense of direction established.

Strategic and tactical plans

Strategic plans, somewhat like long-range plans, deal with the establishment of organizational goals and the development of policies to achieve these goals, whereas tactical plans refer to specific methods for reaching these goals. In military parlance, the strategic aims would be to win the war or a certain campaign; the tactical maneuvers would focus on specific battles or engagements.

Assume that a large insurance company wants to move into the malpractice insurance field and, within a given number of years, intends to dominate this field. All of this it wants to accomplish without reducing the profitability of existing programs. These are goals, or strategic plans. The tactics, then, would be to describe ways to move toward dominance — a competitive rate structure, augmented sales force, attractive printed materials and sales tools, exhibits at health-related conventions, and wide publicity — particularly in medical journals, personal communication with medical leaders, and a massive advertising campaign.

One-time plans and standing plans

Some plans have a single, limited purpose — to celebrate a centennial or to produce a documentary film. Once the end is attained, the plan may be dissolved. Thus, the one-time plan serves an ongoing function.

Standing plans, on the other hand, encompass management policies, standard operating procedures, and institutional or company rules.

Policies are general guidelines to assist in decision-making. They could cover anything from proper attire to emergency leave.

Procedures explain how things are to be done, particularly things that occur with some frequency. Public relations departments may have a regular system for answering complaints, acknowledging donors, or preparing a certain executive's speech.

Rules define what should and should not be done in a given situation. A publicity director may have an office rule that all correspondence to media outlets must be personalized. A company may insist that all news items and brochures must clear through the PR office — a good rule, incidentally. Rules may be discarded on occasion, and they are often suspended to meet a unique situation.

OBSTACLES TO PLANNING

Despite the logic and necessity of planning, it is common for communications and events to be poorly planned. The reasons, or excuses, are numerous.

Not enough time

There may not be enough lead time to plan an event properly. Or the practitioner may be so busy "executing" that he or she takes no time to look ahead.

Lack of confidence

The practitioner may take a dim view of the planning process, the organization, or the practitioner's own abilities.

Fear of failure

Some PR people live in fear of having their ideas shut down. They play it safe, insulating themselves against complaints by continual busywork or by failing to bring plans to measurable fruition. This type of person cannot last long in such a visible profession

Resistance to change

A number of executives enjoy the comfort of familiar routines. Their goals are outdated and their methods unimaginative — but they squeak by.

Too much red tape

Steering new concepts through channels may be so complicated that the practitioner doesn't even try. He or she could also be naive about organizational structures and ignorant of the way corporate actions are accomplished.

Failure to understand the present environment

Plans go awry because facts external to the organization were not considered. Several recent advertising campaigns had to be scrapped because they proved offensive to minorities or because they seemed "sexist" to female consumers.

Not enough money or personnel

Overworked executives may conclude that initiating any new program will simply add more work for them, so they sit on innovations. PR persons may feel, too, that the money to support their ideas will never be released so they drop them. The situation could be real or imaginary. Increasing the mail contributions to a charitable institution won't work unless more personnel are added to process the increased returns.

Vague company goals and objectives

Unless the practitioner knows where the company intends to go and how it plans to get there, he or she cannot come up with satisfactory subplans.

Exclusion of PR person from key meetings

Some practitioners are summoned to the executive suite only after a crisis has arisen. No public relations program can function under these conditions. The PR director should insist on being part of the strategy team.

VARIATIONS IN PLANNING

No two circumstances are exactly alike. Organizational structures dictate some differences. So do such things as the nature of the business and the size of the institution or corporation. Small organizations obviously require less complicated planning than large ones do. The whole spectrum of internal and external conditions also influences planning.

Managerial styles vary. Some executives are cautious, even secretive, and confine planning tasks to relatively few people. Others possess a more open, liberal style, involving people at all levels and disseminating results widely.

Subject matter constitutes another variation. The purchasing officer's plans will differ from those of the public relations director. The former will be considering such elements as inventory, unit cost, availability, and future need, while the PR director will be studying target audiences, media response, and communication roadblocks.

There are also differences of opinion on "central planning" versus a design constructed at a lower level. Tom Peters, author of the very successful book, *In Search of Excellence*, comes down in favor of the latter regimen.

. . . large central corporate staffs that generate 35 notebooks, each 300 pages long, are a waste of time. Many give lip service to "the right stuff," like decentralized, bottom-up planning. But look at their apparently innocuous "corporate planning-guidance document" and you'll see that they have carved up space which should have been left to divisions. I'm in favor of sound strategic thinking and a well-drawn plan — at the division level.

Flexibility

Some flexibility should be built into every plan. Nothing will work exactly as diagrammed. Costs may escalate, people may stumble, the environment can alter drastically, and goals may change. Instead of becoming upset when such cogs appear, the professional should be able to shift gears and save at least part of the plan.

Timing

An otherwise good plan may be ahead of its time; people aren't ready for it. It may also be too late; the mood has passed. Knowing exactly when to inaugurate a program takes considerable skill.

Timing in planning is like training in athletics. The runner and the boxer attempt to peak at the race or bout. In the same way, plans are most effective when they reach a somewhat conditioned audience.

Another timing caution is that planners must always allow sufficient time for their objectives to be realized. You can't decide to raise $500,000 on Thursday and schedule a kick-off breakfast for the following Monday.

Appropriateness

Plans should be appropriate to the organization or institution. They must be able to win management's support and should be matched to the resources of the sponsor. More than that, they should also be appropriate in themselves and in terms of the image and goals of the institution. A downtown treasure hunt may be properly sponsored by a merchant's group but may be inappropriate for a cancer research institute. Establishing a scholarship fund for underprivileged students could be good public relations for a corporation but a questionable move for a private hospital.

CHAPTER 4

The Costs of Public Relations

Probably because in some ill-informed quarters a strange idea exists that public relations is free advertising, the reckoning of PR costs is sometimes misunderstood. The costing of PR activities is no different from the costing of anything else comprising labor and materials that are combined with the intention of carrying out a task effectively and economically and, in the case of a consultant, profitably.

Some employers of internal PR staff and a good many consultants have very little idea of the real costs of public relations. It is truly amazing how many employers will turn a conveniently blind eye to overhead expenses, how users of outside services will accept a service with an arbitrarily conceived and seldom ever justified overall fee and, worse still, how many PR consultants abhor timesheets and operate unprofitable consultancy services that are more like charities for selfish clients. Far too many clients literally believe that public relations is free publicity and pay extraordinarily tiny fees, presumably because they cannot conceive of PR work costing much to perform. This remarkably unrealistic state of affairs can only be ended when users of PR services understand what they are buying, what it costs, and what constitutes value for money

There is, nevertheless, a very genuine reason why some users of public relations are confused about costs. They are or were in receipt of very extensive free services from their advertising agents because of the curious commission system, although this is rapidly giving way to various kinds of fee systems.

The commission system, which is convenient to the media owners, really means that the media owners subsidize the account executives, space buyers, production, print buying, progress chasing, and other staff. The commission system not only prevents the advertising agency from making a proper professional charge for work done, but the cost of work is hidden from the client. Consequently, it comes very hard to have to pay for somewhat similar services when carried out by a PR consultancy, and the different method of charging is even more perplexing when it comes from the PR department or subsidiary of the advertising agency whose services are apparently free. In fact, advertising agency owners or PR consultancies do not themselves always appreciate what they should properly charge, and there was a time when some advertising agencies tried — most unprofitably — to throw in PR services as freely as other services, overlooking the fact that this required a heavy subsidy from agency resources.

So, we must start with the assumption that everything must be paid for, and that as PR personnel become better selected, trained, qualified, and experienced, they will be able to command salaries equivalent to those earned by advertising personnel. Inevitably, public relations will cost and be worth more when performed by more competent practitioners. As with advertising, vast progress is likely to occur in a short space of time once PR recruits understand how much they need to learn.

One curiosity of PR costing needs to be disposed of right away, and that is the practice of tacking a little something on to the end of an advertising budget (or deducting it from this budget) for PR. The PR executive is then told he or she has a certain sum for public relations before he or she has had any opportunity to make a study and present proposals. This practice often occurs in advertising agencies where the account executive has no understanding of public relations. This is yet another reason why there should be a separate budget for public relations, and separate negotiations for PR services even when they are to be carried out by a department or subsidiary of the advertising agency.

THE PR BUDGET

Let us now examine the items that constitute a PR budget, looking at this from the points of view of both the staff PR officer and the outside consultant. The four basic elements are:

▶   labor
▶   office overhead
▶   materials
▶   expenses

Labor

Salaries of management and specialist PR staff, salaries of secretarial, clerical, and accountancy staff. Fees to freelance, consultancy, and other outside staff.

Office Overhead

All rent, insurance, light, telecommunications, internet associated fees, office services, client liaison.

Materials

All stationery, photography, postage, print, visual aids, exhibition stands, films, and other items.

Expenses

All out-of-pocket expenses incurred by staff, such as fares, hotel bills, and entertainment of guests, plus catering costs for functions and events.

The consultant will expect to make a gross profit of at least 15 percent and this means charging a service fee capable of recovering salaries and overhead, although some income may be derived from commissions or quantity concessions on certain materials, such as print and photography. Expenses are charged at cost and where these are heavy, as with catering for a press reception, they are best charged directly to the client by the contractor, otherwise they may represent interest-free loans.

There is a somewhat old-fashioned argument that it is unprofessional for a PR consultant to accept fees from suppliers, but the consultant who handles films, house journals, and exhibitions may well depend on these fees for a major part of his income. The amount of consulting or counseling done by the average consultant may occupy only a minor part of the time or work load with the most of it occurring in the original planning stages and then at subsequent progress meetings. The bulk of the fee will be taken up by the time expended on carrying out the program. Few consultancy fees can be regarded as retainers for PR advice, although such an item can, and should, be specifically written into a consultant's budget proposals.

The client may say he or she can operate a PR department and save the consultant's profit, but the client can do this only when he or she would otherwise be employing a PR consultancy full-time or more than full-time, and if he or she is conveniently situated as a consultant. It has to be recognized that although the consultant may have to bear and charge the overhead expenses of an office in the center of a city, compared with the lower cost of an office in a suburb, the cost of sharing those city facilities is a very modest investment in more efficient PR services.

The false argument occurs when the client resents paying consultancy fees and thinks that for a smaller or even the same outlay, the client could run its own PR department. The client cannot, of course, run an effective PR department on this sort of outlay for two reasons:

- ▶ If the client is paying a consultant a small fee, he or she is using only a proportion of an executive's time and, consequently, if the client employed a PR officer full-time, the officer would have to indulge in extra PR activity that might well incur numerous other costs, such as house journals, films, seminars, work visits, and so on. This, in turn, would probably involve further expenditure on additional salaries.

- ▶ While a staff PR officer and secretary may be engaged for the cost of their salaries, they still have to be housed, equipped, serviced, and supplied with other services. And since the additional volume of work is bound to require additional staff, such as a PR assistant and secretary with their own overhead, it is unlikely that an internal PR department comparable with a PR consultancy service can be undertaken more economically. It may be undertaken differently or more efficiently, but that is another matter associated with the intimacy of in-house public relations. It can therefore be misleading to compare consultancy costs with PR department costs.

COST OF INTERNAL PR DEPARTMENT

Let us now look more closely at the costs that concern the internal PR unit, assuming that the internal unit is at least an embryo PR department consisting of a public relations officer or manager and secretary.

Labor

The staff of a PR department may include all of the following personnel:

- ▶ Public relations officer
- ▶ Exhibition manager
- ▶ Public relations specialist
- ▶ Events organizer
- ▶ House journal editor
- ▶ Support staff
- ▶ Films and photography officer

▶ General office staff

▶ Internet and media relations specialist

▶ Web assistance

The budget must therefore include their salaries, pension funds, insurance, and taxes as may be appropriate under current policy or legislation, and successive budgets must allow for bonuses and salary increases.

Each organization's PR department will vary according to its particular needs, and two seemingly identical companies serving much the same market could undertake public relations in very different ways. This is the great advantage of public relations over advertising as a means of communications since public relations can adopt more than one method with equal effectiveness. However, in a sizable PR campaign, the house journal and the documentary film will both occupy important places in the program, but a smaller campaign could use either one or the other. (It will be inferred from these remarks that press relations is already being relegated to just a place in a program, and not the whole program itself, as it is sometimes regarded.)

A modest PR department will therefore consist of at least a PR officer, a media relations specialist, and web assistant(s).

Costs could be lessened if the more specialist duties were supplied by outside PR consultants, photographers, film producers, exhibition stand designers, house journal producers, and others. It is by no means a case of making a distinct choice between either an internal department or a consultancy; many sensible and valuable combinations are possible, and these combinations are an important aspect of PR costing. For example, it is pointless maintaining even a two-person film unit unless at least three films per year are to be made or, again, unless the film unit can double on other duties, photographic or otherwise. There is no point in investing in idleness of employees.

There is, however, a contributory aspect of public relations that can seldom be budgeted accurately, although some allowance should be made when the cost would otherwise have to be met out of PR department salaries. Here we mean all the innumerable PR activities that the PR officer may inspire but which a PR-oriented management that recognizes that public relations is something implicit in the proper management and conduct of any organization may well instigate.

With this in mind, it is difficult to understand the thinking of those who regard public relations as a luxury. All that is new is the integration, planning, and control of the relations that an organization inevitably has with its numerous publics. A PR department in a civic center can be a genuine investment capable of saving taxpayer money and making local government more efficient and better understood by the people whom it serves. The classic example for the need for public relations was the way in which rate rebates for those with small incomes — mainly poor, elderly folk — was totally mishandled by British local authorities unwilling to use PR, so that a Labor government had to indulge in a costly series of TV commercials.

The PR-conscious organization will therefore operate through PR-minded executives or officials, and their staffs, in every department. Good relations is often no more than good manners. In an industrial organization, the factory manager, human resources manager, maintenance engineer, warehouse manager, transportation manager, and other departmental heads can all contribute by creating and maintaining good relations with their respective publics. To these may be added branch, area, and field managers who may be in charge of retail outlets, depots, or sales offices. Their PR costs are difficult to place in the PR budget, and the recognized cost of an organization's public relations may be related only to the central inspiration through the staff house journal, online publication, internal memos, staff meetings, and conferences, and possibly by means of film, videotape, or Power Point presentations. The internal role of the staff PR officer must never be overlooked.

In local government, this sort of thing is even more apparent because much of the success of a local authority PR officer's work will depend not only on the cooperation he or she obtains from the committees and committee chair people, but especially from fellow local government officers. A major cost of local government public relations is the time spent on integrating the PR requirements of a very complex organization that has a crying need for communication with its publics. Nowhere is PR more seriously needed than in establishing communication between local government service and the taxpayers. Since the majority of taxpayers never enter its door, it is not enough to look upon the public library as an official information service.

Office Overhead

A PR department requires more than just offices for executives and secretaries; it is very much a workshop requiring working areas for assembling, packing, designing, and generating production materials. This is expensive. Once again, it may be cheaper to use a consultant who has all these facilities. An organization cannot expect to undertake its own public relations unless it is prepared to devote a sufficient slice of office accommodation to its PR staff.

The location of the PR office is also important, and ideally it should be in a principal city, in close proximity to communication media and other facilities, and preferably centralized. This can mean a high office rent, but this should not be shirked when there is a serious intention to set up a fully operative PR department. However, the PR office should not be isolated from the main center of production and employment as frequent visits may be necessary. PR staff should maintain good communication with the entire organization, even if it has scattered locations — this could involve installing additional direct lines, fax machines, computers, or having a press officer in each location.

As a result of this argument, it can be seen that office overhead should include the cost of maintaining contact with the local branches, offices, factories, mines, or mills, wherever they may be located in the country or overseas. The PR department cannot be fully operative unless it is a central hive of information — the eyes and ears of the organization. Normal office overhead will also include rent, heat, electricity, telecommunications, cleaning, and other service charges. It is essential that these be included, and the PR officer should not be housed in a couple of spare offices free of charge so that no real cost is budgeted.

Materials

PR work has its own creative and production costs. A story may be published free of charge in a magazine, as it deserves to be if it is genuine news, but it is not produced free of cost. As already stated, salaries and office overhead have to be allocated. Now, one must consider the materials used by the workers in the office.

The following is a list of some of the items that come under this heading:

▶ Envelopes for news releases, photographs (card backed), correspondence, brochures, etc.

▶ Letterhead

▶ Printed news release paper

▶ Photograph caption blanks, preferably printed with identification details

▶ Invitation cards for press receptions

▶ Press kits

▶ Duplicating materials

▶ Suitable binders, files, etc., for press clips, photographic records plus normal office supplies

▶ Computer and word processing services

The above list can be adapted or extended according to the special needs of the organization, which may require other materials such as prints of films, all kinds of printed materials, blow-ups of pictures, video, slides, charts, and other visual aids, and the various materials required by specialist staff, including house journal editors, photographers, film/digital producers, exhibition designers, and event organizers.

Expenses

This is an item that has to be realistically anticipated and rigorously controlled. Lavish expenditure is stupid. If staff are expected to give up their spare time and be separated from their homes and families, they deserve the compensation for first-class travel, decent meals, and first-class accommodation.

Expenses are likely to include the following items:

▶ Automobile expenses, either supplying vehicles or paying a mileage rate

▶ Fares

▶ Overnight hotel expenses

▶ Meals while traveling

▶ Entertainment of visitors, contacts

▶ Catering expenses for press receptions, seminars, other PR events

▶ Rent for halls and equipment such as microphones and projectors

▶ Hiring of transportation — cars, vans, coaches, trains, aircraft

▶ Supply of newspapers, trade magazines, yearbooks, directories

The expenses will obviously vary according to whether one is mainly producing technical articles about installations, for instance, or doing something more elaborate, such as producing an exhibition.

CHAPTER 5

Presentation of a News Release

There are two aspects to the production of a successful news release. One is the way it is presented and the other is the way it is written. Although the presentation is largely a matter of designing and duplicating what has already been written by hand or on computer, the author should have the final appearance in mind at the creative stage. The author will then apply techniques that are logical, and therefore essential, if a publishable news release is to be produced. The author will restrict capital letters to proper names and write the article in clear English. A news release (or an article) has to be set out as a manuscript and not as a business letter. Judging by the appearance of many news releases put out, this is unknown to most secretaries and administrative assistants.

Therefore, let us analyze the basic presentation very carefully. A first-class press officer will be meticulous over these details.

The purpose of good, correct presentation is threefold:

▶ to achieve legibility

▶ to make the release attractive to read and newsworthy

▶ to minimize editorial work so that the release is capable of publication as it stands

The less a story is cut or rewritten, the less likelihood there is of its meaning being changed. Having said that, however, it must be admitted that while a trade magazine may print the story exactly as submitted by the press officer, a major newspaper will invariably do a rewrite job to suit its own style and may well use the news release merely as a piece of information on which to base a story resulting from further investigation. In both cases, however, it is essential that the press officer issue information in a thoroughly professional manner, and this really boils down to presenting the facts as an editor would like to receive them.

These three requirements therefore imply a knowledge of human psychology and an appreciation for editorial needs. Unfortunately, many news releases fail to meet these three elementary requirements. The presentation of a news release is as much a piece of marketing as the packing of a shirt in a plastic bag and a nice box.

ESSENTIAL ELEMENTS OF PRESENTATION

The presentation can be divided into the following 9 elements:

▶ The basic sheet

▶ Length, ending, and authorship

▶ Headlines, subheads and paragraphs

▶ Style and punctuation

▶ Embargoes and dating

▶ Picture availability

▶ Layout

▶ Printing

▶ Assembling

The basic sheet

Sheet size. A standard letter size sheet of paper has become the universally accepted paper size for news release. An advantage of this size sheet is that it makes it very easy to restrict the majority of news stories to the ideal of one piece of paper, a distinct advantage from the point of view of a busy editor. It is always psychologically easier to induce someone to read what is presented to them on one side of a single piece of paper.

The printed heading

A news release that is merely duplicated straight onto plain paper without a printed heading looks dull and amateurish. A printed news release heading should quickly establish the identity of the sender. When a reputation has been won for good, interesting, and accurate press stories, instant recognition by means of a distinctive heading will be a desirable asset since the editor of even a small trade paper may receive as many as 50 or more different news releases of varying length in a single day. A news release heading should simply distinguish that it is not a business letter or an advertisement heading. The wording should clearly state the name, address, telephone number, and fax number (if there is one), and email address for further information, and a night or home telephone number can be helpful.

A PR consultancy has the problem of declaring the identities of both itself and its client, but from the editor's point of view, it is the client's identity that matters even though further information is to be had from a consultant. It is therefore wrong, if common, for the consultant's name to predominate. In fact, it is best if the sender's identification is printed discreetly at the foot of the sheet, the only print at the top being perhaps a single word such as **NEWS**, or **INFORMATION**, or possibly **NEWS RELEASE**.

The effect is to give emphasis to the story, and since the story is reproduced in black it would contrast very legibly with neat, informative but unobtrusive colored print. Moreover, since the subject of the news release will be clear from the headline and the opening words, this style of release heading is self-identifying insofar as the client or organization is concerned.

Length, ending, and authorship

The question of length occurs many times. The more concise and precise the release is, the more readable and acceptable it is likely to be. Nevertheless, with very technical products it may be proper to cover the subject in sufficient depth to make the story worth publishing. Discretion must be applied according to the topic and the media. However, here we are concerned with length from the point of view of presentation, and length can sometimes be determined at the preparation stage because if a second sheet is going to be required to carry a continuation of only a few lines, it is usually possible to cut the story in order to keep it to a single piece of paper.

Finally, there is the question of editorial time and editorial needs. Editors receive so many hundreds of PR stories every week that they simply do not have the time to wade through pages of verbosity. The news agencies, which generally put out wire stories of no more than 80 words, despair at the daily arrival of long-winded news releases that doom themselves on sight.

Thus, when the facts are presented as briefly as possible, and the story can be read almost at a glance, there is seldom any need to go beyond the ample space provided by a single letter-size sheet.

The editing of the release and its authorship are related to the length, and particularly to the more detailed release that does run to more than one sheet.

All news releases should close with the name of the writer. This is important when the story has been organized and transmitted from a consultancy, less necessary when it has come from an organization whose press officer is named on the printed heading. Closing the story with the author's name is a clear way of finishing and a good way of establishing personal contact and responsibility for the facts.

Headlines, subheads, and paragraphs

Here there are three elements of a news release about which there seems to be hardly any agreed-upon standard practice. However, when ordinary editorial needs are considered, there can surely be no question about the required practice if good press relations are to be maintained. Let us examine each one of these in turn.

HEADLINES

Although it is tempting to invent clever, alternative headlines, no one will use them. Each editor likes to Write one's own, unless one is lazy or there is no better alternative to the one submitted. The purpose of the news release headline is to quickly identify the story. The headline, which is not to be confused with the printed heading already discussed, has a practical purpose, yet it may never be printed if only because editors do not want to print the same headlines as their rivals. Sometimes, employers and clients try to insist that the press officer should word the headline in some dramatic or persuasive manner, but the press officer must dissuade them from doing this, as an advertisement-type headline suggests to some editors that the content will be the same. The headline should therefore create the right impression that what follows is a genuine, factual, news story.

While the foregoing is sound standard practice, there can be occasion when the story of a seemingly dull or difficult subject can be given a lift and marketed by a bright and possibly humorous treatment.

SUBHEAD

Again, it is tempting to insert subheadings to add interest to a story, but they may be a nuisance to the editor who either does not use them or likes to insert them where they suit him or her. So it is best not to use subheads except in very long releases that have clear-cut sections dealing with separate items, such as a number of different models. Even then, it may be better to write individual releases on each subject rather than bury the various items in an omnibus story. However, common sense must prevail. In all these matters, the press officer has to remember that this story will be going to many editors who will each have distinctive styles of presentation. Therefore, it is wise to present the basic story as clearly as possible, leaving each editor to set out it out as he or she pleases. If the press officer knows that a publication prefers subheads, it is best to use them.

PARAGRAPHS

Some press officers do not clearly understand the use of paragraphs and their presentation, but the lesson can be learned very quickly by studying the columns of daily newspapers. Modern journalism calls for short paragraphs. They help people to read quickly and absorb the message clearly. Short paragraphs can be deliberately used to keep the interest flowing.

The setting out of paragraphs is not limited to their length, however. Most newspapers and magazines indent all paragraphs except the first, and news releases should adhere to this style. It is called book style. A news story with unindented paragraphs is a nuisance in that it requires just that extra bit of attention.

Style and punctuation

CAPITAL LETTERS

Capital letters belong to titling or to proper names. Indiscriminate use of capital letters can be the bane of an editor's life. A company or product name should never be written entirely in capitals, nor should initial capitals be used for nouns.

> *"The new range of central heating equipment made by ABC Ltd. includes Solid Fuel, Gas-fired, and Oil-fired Boilers."*

It should be set like this:

> *"The new range of central heating equipment made by ABC Ltd. includes solid fuel, gas-fired, and oil-fired boilers."*

Far too many news releases are written in needless capitals and it is plain to see the extent of editorial correction that becomes necessary.

Technical people are apt to refer to Cocoa, Radar, Timber, Steel, Businesspeople, Directors, Boards, Annual General Meetings, and Dividends, but these capital letters are incorrectly used and must not be used in a news release.

Nor should emphasis be given by typing passages in capitals. All emphasis should be left to the editor since it is not the place of the press officer to comment or invite testimony. The author of the news release must content him or herself with supplying factual materials free of bias. Otherwise, the news release becomes an advertisement. This distinction is sometimes, and understandably, difficult to appreciate by advertising people when they are employing press relations services.

UNDERLINING AND QUOTATION MARKS

As a general rule, no underlining should appear anywhere in a news release, and preferably not even in the headline. It is no business of the press officer to stipulate which words should be set in italics, except in the case of foreign words or Latin names in scientific matter. The academic style of underlining book titles, however, does apply to news releases.

Similarly, quotation marks should generally be avoided. The time to use quotation marks is when actual speech or material from another source is being quoted verbatim, always remembering that it is necessary to place quotation marks at the beginning of each paragraph and to conclude the entire speech or quotation with quotation marks. Otherwise, it is not absolutely clear where the quote starts and finishes. An organization official may be quoted in the news release.

NUMERALS AND SYMBOLS

A paragraph should never begin with a numeral unless a list of points is being made, and if the sentence cannot be restructured satisfactorily, the numeral must be spelled out. Except in special cases, numbers from one to nine should be spelled out, after which numerals such as 59 and 101 should be used until the numbers become so unwieldy that it is clearer to spell out many thousands rather than 5,000,000 or $5,000,000. The actual numerals should be given in dates, June 1st and not June first, and 2010, not two thousand ten. The press officer has to be extremely careful that accurate and easily understood figures are given in news releases. An error can be disastrous once it is printed, and little can be done by way of correction. If the story has been widely distributed the error may be perpetuated for weeks, months, even years.

The same applies to measurements and symbols where there is any risk of a mistake. It is advisable to avoid the symbols and write 90 degrees and 100 percent.

While on the subject, it is all too easy to be lax about the use of figures, symbols, and punctuation, and inconsistencies such as four-wheel and 4-wheel are surprisingly frequent in the same press release. In the short space of a few hundred words, the press officer should be capable of repeating numerical facts in the same way.

A symbol that is badly abused is the ampersand (&), which should never appear in a sentence unless it is part of the normal way of spelling a company name. At best, it is a lazy device, sometimes resorted to by those who write quickly in longhand. The ampersand has its uses where space is scarce — that is, in headlines and tabulated matter such as lists, catalogs, and accounts.

FULL POINTS OR FULL STOPS

Periods should not be used between initial abbreviations such as BSc, BBC, MCC, and so on. If they were inserted — viz.: B.Sc., B.B.C., M.M.C. — the effect would be a spotty mess. Needless editorial work can again be eliminated by the omission of these periods in the first place. This absence of periods in abbreviations is common to all types of publications, and although exception can be found, the appearance of the text is always improved when the periods are omitted.

Periods remain a vital form of punctuation, however, and the so-called letter-writing style that omits all punctuation must not be used when preparing a news release.

PUNCTUATION

Generally, the clarity of a news story can depend upon use of punctuation, and commas, colons, semicolons, dashes, and brackets are the signposts of written communication. The pedantic use of punctuation can impede reading, but the lack of essential punctuation can cause misunderstanding. Sometimes punctuation is omitted through carelessness, and all copy must be scrutinized to see that parentheses are completely and correctly punctuated.

Embargoes and Dating

The date when a story may be published, the use of dates in stories, and the date when the release is issued are three things of great consequence to the recipient of press releases.

EMBARGOES

An embargo is an instruction to the press that the story should not be published before a certain date and perhaps even a certain time on that date. There are many occasions when an embargo is vital, and this is often so in financial public relations or when stories are being issued in different parts of the world where disparity in times could cause embarrassment if publication took place literally at the same time. The announcement of price changes or the publication of a speech are typical examples where it can be very helpful if an editor can have the news well in advance provided he or she respects the privilege and does not print the speech before it has been delivered.

But having admitted the necessity for embargoes, it must be emphasized that embargoes should be used sparingly and sensibly. Long embargoes, though, are bad and hardly ever justified. They usually have the effect of killing interest in the story. An embargo should be a privilege, enabling the editor to have advance knowledge or information that would be foolish or improper to publish before the stipulated date and time. For example, political correspondents receive advance copies of speeches, the contents of which they must not divulge prematurely. However, if an embargo is unexpected and irrelevant, it may even get overlooked.

Most stories should therefore be for immediate release and if that is so, it is pointless to print *"for immediate release"* across the top, unless it comes from one of those rare organizations that seldom issue a story without a stringent embargo. One suspects that some of the releases from commercial sources which bear dramatic embargoes or permissions for instant publication are produced by somewhat amateurish writers who are trying to capture some of the supposed glamour of a hectic newsroom.

DATES

If a date is important to the story, it should be included in the narrative, and the month should be read first and be spelled out in full, thus: November 12, 2010. The month, which is generally more significant and memorable than the day of the month, should be placed first. This significance is further borne out by the fact that press reports often refer to months only. Vague reference to "today," "yesterday," "tomorrow," or "recently" must be replaced by the actual date. Reliance should not be placed on the date of the release itself.

If the release describes a stand at an exhibition, the headline should state all the relevant details about the name of the exhibition, venue, dates, hall, and stand number. In large cities, there are many exhibitions taking place every week and editors cannot be expected to know when and where every exhibition is being held.

It should not be necessary for an editor to have to phone the press officer and ask, "When did it happen?" Moreover, dated stories should be issued promptly so that their news value is not lost, and this implies knowing the last date or even time deadline for copy for different types of publications. It may be that it is too late to write, reproduce, and distribute a news release and that telephone, telex, fax, email, or one of the press services, such as Associated Press, will have to dispatch the story.

DATING RELEASES

Apart from dates that are part of the information supplied, releases themselves should be dated. Some press officers insert the date at the beginning of the first page with a dark rule. A consultant will also find it useful to combine the job number with the date in a coding at the foot of the page. However, this is not necessarily explicit to an editor unless the month is spelled out, thus: XYZ1001/October 12, 2010. There are, therefore, at least two methods of dating releases:

▶ at the beginning, as with dating a letter (use a date line)

▶ combined with a coding system that is useful for other purposes

Whichever method is chosen, dating is important to prevent out-of-date information being published as can happen with magazines that file releases for future use.

Picture availability

It may not be feasible to send photographs with every news release issued as this would be costly and wasteful. But the availability of pictures can be stated on the release, and since this is not publishable information, these details should be set apart from the body of the story — that is, below the author's name. (Alternatively, the pictures can be identified and described on an accompanying order form.) Photo captions should not be incorporated in news releases — they must be attached to the actual prints.

Layout

SPACING

All manuscript work should be double or single-and-a-half spaced in proportion to the size of the font on the computer.

MARGINS

A right-hand as well as left-hand margin is needed in a press release, although this is not typical with general manuscript work for articles and books. Both margins should not be less than 1.5 inches (4 cm) to allow for editorial comment.

CONTINUATION

When the news release consists of more than one sheet of paper, this should be clearly indicated at the foot of the page, and all succeeding pages should be numbered. If this is done, more elaborate continuation references are redundant. Use of the word *"more"* is convenient when a story is being produced in a number of loose sheets, as may happen in a newspaper office.

Printing

All manuscript work must be typed or duplicated on one side of the paper only, and anything on the reverse side will be ignored. Editors and publishers always work from material on one side of the paper only.

Assembling

As already stated, the ideal news story is one that is confined to one sheet of paper; however, there are times when a story does run to two or three pages. There are different ways to joining sheets together. The paper clip is dangerous and can come adrift in a pile of editorial material on the editor's desk. The most suitable is the small wire staple, provided it is properly depressed. When folding the release for insertion in the envelope, the stapled end should be enclosed within the folds, otherwise there is risk that the metal will rip the envelope during its postage through the mail, or damage accompanying photographs.

It is also important to fold cleanly to avoid unnecessary bulk that can spring open a poorly sealed envelope. If mailings are done frequently, a folding machine is a good investment, and there are several models on the market that handle work of various complexities. In today's marketplace, most press releases are sent by email or electronic distribution services.

This is possibly a good point at which to warn the press officer that administrative assistants are not always aware of the rough handling that postal packages have to suffer. Unless items are securely packed and sealed, they will stand little chance of surviving the hazards of the postal service. The onus is on the sender to protect whatever is mailed.

Envelopes: A Technical Section

The release should be folded as few times as possible so that it is as presentable as possible on arrival. There is no point in folding a standard letter sheet so that it will squeeze into a small business envelope. A standard letter needs to be folded only twice to fit an ordinary #10 size envelope. A bulkier release, or a feature article, is best folded only once and posted in a larger envelope.

However, when accompanying a half-plate photograph (the size least likely to get damaged in the mail by the string that postmen tie around bundles of letters for any one address) the release has to be folded once each way for insertion in a suitable envelope. A single sheet news release is preferable with a photograph so that there is no danger of damage from the metal staple.

It is a simple matter to draw up a brief version of these recommendations and to see that every member of the press office staff has a copy to stick on the wall if need be.

It is a mistake for press officers to add a note at the end of the story requesting a press clipping if the story is printed and it is unnecessary to enclose a cover letter urging the editor to print the story. Many editors are generous about sending press clippings or, better still, actual copies of the journal, but it is rather tactless to ask editors for favors. An exception, however, may be when the story is sent overseas and it is doubtful whether a press clipping will come through a press clipping agency. When dispatching news releases, a copy of the story and, if possible, a copy of the mailing list should be sent to the press clipping agency.

The best advice on the presentation of releases is to look at actual printed stories and see how they are presented.

THE SEVEN-POINT FORMULA FOR WRITING NEWS RELEASES

The following seven points form a logical sequence for the presentation of facts in a news release. The formula is also a useful guide to the sort of information without which a story cannot be written, and as a check list to ensure that a story contains all the necessary factual elements.

With the aid of this formula, a rough draft release can be produced very quickly. Inability to base a release on this formula will immediately reveal the inadequacy of the material on which the writer is trying to produce a story. Poorly written stories, using many words to say very little, are the result of not using such a formula or plot. Here, then, are the seven points to follow:

- ▶ The subject of the story
- ▶ The name of the organization
- ▶ The location of the organization (which may be different from the address for further information)
- ▶ The advantage of the policy, plan, action, product, or service
- ▶ The applications to which the subject may be put
- ▶ The details of specifications, prices, colors, sizes, and so on
- ▶ The source of further information, samples, price lists, or address of showroom or information center of the maker

It is important to determine if the 5Ws have been used to write the news release: Who, what, where, when, why (and how). Journalists use this method for writing news stories and it is still the bible for journalism.

CHAPTER 6

Media Relations

For the corporate sector, communication with media is potentially one of the most effective ways of getting its message across. Media need — and indeed welcome — editorial inputs from business and industry. In return, they provide an avenue through which a company can reach a broad, general audience. Media play an important role in promoting or retarding the growth of the corporate sector. A distorted exposure in the press can do incalculable harm to an organization and even materially alter its business prospects. A company's reputation has a significant impact on its stock market valuation and the morale of its work force. It affects a company's ability to recruit and retain good staff, especially for management positions.

It affects productivity, marketing efforts, and a host of other factors essential to the successful operation of business. Besides, the reputation of an organization can influence a decision about restrictive legislation. It can also create a climate of public sentiment in which such legislation is politically thwarted or even considered.

There is a growing awareness in the corporate sector today about its balanced exposure in the press. An organization may, of course, remain indifferent to the need for a planned interaction with the press. But if its activities impinge on the public interest in any way, the press will publish reports and remarks on the organization without caring much for its cooperation. Some corporate managers still seem to believe that business operations are difficult enough without adding to it the task of frequent communication with the press. If a public relations executive tries to emphasize the need to develop a mutually beneficial relationship with the press, he or she is often told that the chief executive has other things to think about, that the CEO's concern is about results, not popularity.

An organization is perceived by people in a variety of ways, depending upon the messages it transmits, consciously or unconsciously. Unwillingness to communicate invariably foments rumor and speculation. What the company may refuse to disclose, many people (even some with an ulterior motive) are ready to reveal, distort, and even invent. Over the past decade, the reach and influence of the media have increased beyond measure. It has also grown in complexity and become more specialized. In this increasingly complex world, there are thousands of organizations, individuals, and interests clamoring for attention. One can penetrate all the uproar and distraction and deliver the message to the widest possible range of people only by developing a close relationship with media. Good media relations are of far greater value than all the expensive advertisements put together.

The primary goal of media relations is to create a close understanding between the media and the corporate sector. But close understanding does not mean that the press will publish only what the company wants to see in print. No one can expect media to become a forum for handout journalism, at least not in a democracy. But many top executives regard reporters as antagonistic and ill-informed individuals who intend to tear down the business structure. They are generally distrustful of journalists occasionally, perhaps with good reason. They may have had bad experiences with reporters in the past. For some, a feeling of fear and mistrust may be instinctive.

Indeed, many organizations, suffering from loss of public confidence often lay the blame on misrepresentation by the media, claiming that media report only the bad and controversial about them, never the good. Journalists cater primarily to the interests of the readers and there is obviously greater demand for the stories that sell papers. It is a fact of life that people prefer bad news to good. To attract the maximum audience, media emphasize the exceptional rather than the representative. Given the system in which the media operate, one has to expect these anomalies.

The media, as gatekeepers, control the flow of information that reaches the society at large. Cooperation with media, therefore, is a very important aspect of public relations. Today, the term *media relations* is increasingly used to describe the activity once regarded as press relations, reflecting the growing importance of radio broadcasting and television and the internet. There is an increasing appreciation today that good media relations can bring the organization's marketing and corporate objectives into sharper focus before the society at large. A regular flow of information between the media and the corporate sector can also ensure that rival business groups, discontented employees, and unions not be the sole source of information on a critical issue. The company's point of view must also receive adequate consideration.

Traditionally, the relationship between media and public relations has swung subtly between the two opposite extremes of total cooperation and utter hostility. It has been the conventional wisdom that press and public relations people are adversaries. Journalists feel besieged by hordes of public relations people who dump on their desks self-serving stories that have little news value. Public relations people, on the other hand, feel journalists know little about the complexities of their organizations. They are whimsical people who would expose rather than explain.

The apparent conflict of interest between media and public relations probably results from the fact that while one is serving the interest of the paper (or listeners/viewers at large), the other is serving the interest of their organization. But public relations, in our country, has grown professionally over the years in its approach to media. Media, too, increasingly appreciate the role of public relations as a source for potential stories.

The relationship, from the position of being mere friends or adversaries, has become more professional today, based on an understanding of each other's needs. Public relations seeks to explain and interpret truthfully policies and programs of the organization to the media. The media, in their turn, understand that public relations professionals can provide them with information of wider popular interest about the industry. Today, the two functions are closely interdependent and complementary. Both have tasks and, though they may sometimes conflict, more often the generation of news and gathering of news coincide.

Public relations today is an ally of the media in its quest for corporate news. Similarly, most journalists are professionally competent in their task of making a balanced report within the limitations of space and the pressure for an angle that excites. Some will explain that news, which by definition is a departure from the norm, is rarely created by the public relations department. But when industrial chemistry produces an event worth reporting, the information needs of the press are not only considerably important, but also immediate. It can turn to public relations, in all such cases, as a source of news.

Press and public relations today are fellow communicators with different agenda. As long as each understands and appreciates the other's goals, the relationship can be productive for both sides. The first step to successful media relations involves understanding the media, how they work, and what their requirements are. The second is, of course, to relate this knowledge to the functioning of the organization. Journalists constantly look for material that is topical, accurate, relevant, fresh, and, ideally, exclusive or with a special angle.

Their acid test for any news material is:

Will this interest an average reader or viewer?

Therefore, to get better and more frequent exposure in the media, thinking should be attuned to the requirements of the editors, broadcast producers, and cyberspace journalists. This can be easily developed by closely following the types of stories they publish or broadcast, getting an insight into their readership profile, and appreciating their interests and needs.

Failure to understand how the media work — not being aware of deadlines, news values, and beats — can be a severe constraint in maintaining a mutually beneficial relationship. It is only by way of continuous comparison of the treatment of different types of news in various media that insight is provided into why one newspaper dismisses a major item in a single paragraph while another makes it a lead.

Earning confidence

To develop a professionally meaningful relationship, one must be honest in gathering and writing news, and as quick and open with the negative items as with the positive ones. Seasoned media people are always sensitive to any tendency to manipulate information for the benefit of those in power. An evasive answer to a relevant question will make the reporter more inquisitive and more determined to dig out facts. Offering "no comments" is invariably interpreted as an effort to hide something. In most cases, it only confirms their worst suspicions.

Competent journalists will be critically probing. It is futile and unprofessional to ask a reporter to kill a story, however damaging to the organization. All that one can ask for — and should — is a chance to include the organization's point of view on the matter as well. In other words, one may only try to ensure that the organization's worst story receives the best hearing.

The best policy for organizations is, therefore, one of easy approachability and ready communication. A public relations executive should always be available to the media to clarify or verify, especially when the news is bad. Accessibility, when the going is rough, is a quality admired by the media. Cooperation when the media want to talk will more than pay for itself at times when the organization wants to talk to the media. Even in unusual situations like strikes or accidents, it always pays to state the facts with honesty, accuracy, and proper perspective.

Public relations is expected to act as a catalyst, and not a filter, for the company's communication with the media. One can certainly make a case for their organization as powerfully as possible, but must also realize the responsibility of the reporter to write a balanced story. However, the right of the media does not translate to the right to trample over privacy and trust. Moreover, media have the right to be wrong in their opinion, but not the right to be wrong in their facts.

Open door policy

A reporter values a good story above anything else and highly appreciates any professional assistance to that end. As an experienced journalist observed: "The role of public relations, as it pertains to the news media, is to provide us with factual information, either self-generated or upon our request, dealing with the products or services of their employer. That has to be all about it. You provide the information, you provide the facts!"

If there is a call from a journalist, one must make certain the message is taken, then note his or her name, the paper represented, the details of the information sought, how soon an answer is needed, and the reporter's telephone number. Any temptation or pressure to reply at once without much thinking should be resisted. It is quite reasonable then to call back with the answers in a short while. This allows for necessary time to check the facts, draft a few answers, and think through the implications of the questions and the consequences of the answers. The call must always be returned. Journalists working on a story appreciate a call back as soon as possible, even if only to explain that some unforeseen obstacle prevents one from giving a full answer. At all costs, a response like "No comment" or "I am not prepared to talk about this" should be avoided. There is no better way to fuel suspicion and misunderstanding.

Public relations has been described as the art of making friends when you don't need them. Regular contact with correspondents and keeping them apprised of various aspects of the industry — not necessarily for immediate publication — is always appreciated. Contact should be maintained with newspapers at several levels — at the reporter level, at the special correspondent level, and at the assistant editor level.

The media comprise numerous publications. This encompasses a wide range, from general interest newspapers and financial press to specialized journals, including the trade press. Something newsworthy happens within any big organization at regular intervals. A slot may always be found in any of these media to highlight such a development.

In order to be useful to the media, a public relations executive should be able to offer such information to the media in ready-to-publish form. To do this successfully, one has to research the everyday operations of the organization and be savvy to new ways of dealing with old information. Indeed, if one knows the problems and prospects of the industry and feeds the media suitable material for filing authoritative reports and making knowledgeable comments, one will always be sought after. To unearth possible stories, one should have free interaction with employees of the organization at all levels. They may provide the PR executive with story tips, unnoticed otherwise.

To sum up, good press relations seeks to make the journalists' job easy. It means giving media news of wide public interest, conveniently packaged and delivered in good time. Apart from press releases, journalists may be invited to speak to senior executives in the organization for a possible story. Features, complete articles, ready-made interviews, and background information may be filed by computer for ready reference and possible use by journalists.

All the following areas of activity may serve as raw material for news:

▶ Annual production performance

▶ Financial results

▶ Opening of new factory, plant, or office

▶ Takeover bids

▶ Launching of new product or service

▶ Expansion plan

▶ Visits of dignitaries or celebrities

▶ Crisis situation, such as accidents, strikes, etc.

▶ Important orders and exports

▶ Scientific or technical advance in industry

▶ Wage agreement

▶ Signing of a memorandum of understanding

▶ Awards for the organization by national or international bodies

▶ Sponsored events and peripheral welfare activities

▶ Changes in price, product, and services

▶ Appointment of key executives

▶ Specific steps for pollution control

▶ Exhibitions

Razor's edge

Media relations, in the ultimate analysis, is like trading on the razor's edge. It has proved to be a Waterloo for many. One can never be sure that their story will get through, and certainly not in the way desired. There is always something that can go wrong somewhere. But one can, at least, do their best. If balanced coverage is received regularly, one must also be prepared for hard times and take the rough with the smooth. In the process, one should smilingly reconcile to the weird and wonderful ways of the editor's policy, compositor's errors, and occasional sadism of sub-editors. One can work assiduously to offer a journalist good material for a story but if the story comes out in a form entirely different from that anticipated, it would be unwise to jump to the conclusion that the reporter has murdered the story.

Limited space and lack of time sometimes result in broadcasting or printing incomplete or inaccurate news. It is possible that the sub-editors had to drastically reduce the length of the story to make room for other reports. It may also happen that in an effort to give a more catchy angle, the sub-editor had to rewrite the story. Similarly, if the story does not appear at all, it is quite probable that it has been killed in favor of other stories considered to be of greater news value. Sub-editors, in a way, form the backbone of any newspaper but, at the same time, they have to make hard decisions.

No one can expect news to be continually favorable. A very visible company is also a very vulnerable one. One has to accept, like a stoic, good days as well as bad. A high profile must always be tempered by modesty and backed up with performance. After too much glare of publicity, one may suddenly discover that there is much truth in the saying, *"One whom the gods wish to destroy, is first made the darling of the media."*

The reporter's job ends when the story is published. There is no accountability for the consequences of the report, except perhaps to the editor or the owner of the paper. The owners of the newspapers generally allow total editorial freedom to the journalists except when their own business and political interests are affected. Public relations managers, on the other hand, have the task of counseling the management or the organization's public on any information relevant to the report. If the report results in an industrial relations problem or a drop in sales or damage to the corporate reputation, the organization may have to deal with the consequences for months or even years.

There are some golden rules that may be followed in dealing with the media and, similarly, there are some that should be avoided. Here are the TEN COMMANDMENTS OF MEDIA RELATIONS.

▶ Help the reporters submit a story. They will always be grateful for stories that are on time, in a suitable form, and accurate.

▶ Be frank, honest, and modest; it builds trust and confidence (in any case, can truth be hidden for long?).

▶ Give all the news — good as well as bad — providing, preferably, a perspective.

▶ Protect exclusives. A person who uncovers a story deserves full credit.

▶ Trust the reporters. Very rarely will one abuse your trust.

▶ Do not plead either to get a story published or to kill it. It is unprofessional and unproductive. The only way to keep unfavorable stories out of the media is to keep situations that produce such stories from taking place.

▶ Do not grumble about minor errors. Many cannot be helped under the pressure of speed in a newspaper.

▶ Do not play favorites. It creates resentment among others.

▶ Do not maintain a high profile unless it is backed by performance and can be sustained over a long period of time.

▶ Do not feel frustrated and complain if the story is not used. The next one may get there.

CHAPTER 7

Organizing Public Relations Events

The organizing of PR events calls for methodical and meticulous planning. Success often depends on experience — the press officer who has organized other kinds of events will find the experience useful. There is a lot of hard work in organizing a PR event.

THE THREE TYPES OF PR EVENTS

First, it should be stated that there are three main types of media events. The loose expression *press conference* is often used in a vague sense to imply any sort of media gathering, whether assembled or conveyed. By *press conference*, *press reception*, and *facility visit*, one refers to gatherings of accelerating complexity. Respectively, the first is a fairly simple affair, the second occupies a larger place and more time and is, consequently, more elaborate, while the third invariably involves travel.

Press conference

A *press conference* is organized like a meeting, the guest being seated to receive an announcement and to ask questions. It may be held in an office, a board room, or a hotel assembly room. Hospitality is usually modest, perhaps tea or coffee served with cookies, or wine and cheese, according to the time of day. A bar is not always necessary. Copies of the announcement will be available in news release form. A press conference is a fairly unpretentious occasion, capable of being called at short notice if the urgency of the news demands it.

The press reception

The success of this type of media event will largely depend on its being much more than a mere drinking occasion. PR has, in the past, gained a regrettable reputation for "overgenerous" hospitality. Contrary to the impression held by some people, most journalists who attend press receptions come in search of a story, not a free drink.

A press reception's success depends on the promise of a story; this is sufficient to attract a good response to the invitation. For this reason, it pays to include a timed program on or with the invitation, although strangely enough this is rarely done. Some invitations do not even state the purpose of the press reception — it is a wonder anyone bothers to accept. A programmed invitation is more likely to attract the journalists who are seriously interested in your subject and best able to give it media coverage.

A typical timetable would include: the initial reception (without formal announcement), initial refreshment according to the time of day, the business of the occasion, and a final period of hospitality including bar and buffet. The business may require guests to be seated, and this session can be in a separate room away from the catering. It may include speeches, demonstrations, a film, and an opportunity for questions to be asked and answered. Those responsible for answering questions should have anticipated the most likely questions and have their facts at the ready. A good question and answer period can do much to create goodwill if speakers are prepared to reply frankly and fully.

A short documentary film or video — not more than 20 minutes — can be a very useful part of the proceeding and should be included if possible, but it must be relevant and recent if not actually current. It may be someone else's film, showing either production of the raw materials or use of the finished article, if the host company does not have a suitable video of its own. For example, a film showing the manufacture of laminates might be shown at a reception for a furniture maker. The documentary or industrial film, free of advertising, is undoubtedly one of the best PR mediums available, and guests at press receptions become most receptive audiences. A video gives information entertainingly and most people enjoy watching them.

If the film is the first item on the program after the reception, it can create a very pleasant atmosphere for the remainder of the party. Platform activities should be rehearsed and timed. A good 20-minute film is infinitely better than a dull 10-minute speech.

It can be a wise plan to separate the business section from the refreshments. The catering bill is doubled when there is no separate business session, and the worst offenders can be the representatives of the host organization (who mistake the event for an opportunity to indulge in some free cocktails with socializing). The organizer should restrict company representatives to essential hosts, such as technical experts needed to talk authoritatively to guests.

Facility visits

Facility visits provide the press with the opportunity, and often the privilege, of attending an official opening, visiting a factory or other premises, visiting an installation, boarding a new ship, flying in a new aircraft, or being taken abroad to an overseas exhibition. For trips, anything from private car to chartered aircraft may be used. These events can be costly because the party has to be conveyed from point to point, fed and entertained, and, on a long trip, overnight accommodation is necessary.

There are two basic kinds of facility visits and the organizer should be clear in the invitation about the kind that is being held. First, there is the visit that is purely to provide background information; second, there is the kind with a definite news story and this will require facilities for some guests to feed the story back by telephone, fax, or email. The press will expect the visit to be of one type or the other. It is foolish to take a planeload of journalists from one end of the country to the other to see a tool or paint factory no different from one they could see in their own local area. Unfortunately, this happens all too often, and public relations gets a bad name for unnecessary extravagance.

The facility visits have been organized so extravagantly on some occasions that the press have their own word for it — *junket* — and this joins the rest of the press world's contemptuous jargon concerning PR. Hollywood's priciest press junket was in the '60s when Twentieth-Century Fox spent a quarter of a million dollars on a week's junket for film cities. First, the press party went to New York for the opening of *The Boston Strangler,* then flew over to Paris to watch the shooting of *The Staircase,* followed by a trip to Tunis to view *Justine,* then returning to Paris for *The Only Game in Town* and the premiere of *A Flea in Her Ear.* This was followed by a dinner party at the famous Maxim's. The week was concluded by a flight to London to see *The Chairman* and finally back to New York to see *Star.*

RADIO AND TV

These three events — conferences, receptions, and visits — are labeled "press" but radio and TV should be considered separately and differently from the print media and from the internet. A common mistake is to include representatives of radio and TV news in the general invitation list. An even greater error is to simply blanket-invite TV and radio without realizing the numerous sections that now exist in radio and television, commercial or otherwise.

Unless reporters from radio and TV are content to "sit in" in search of material for future programs, they should not be sent a general invitation to attend a press event. Instead, after careful selection of the appropriate programs and stations, the respective producers, presenters, or reporters should be written to or telephoned individually. This should be done in advance of the general press invitations. Broadcasters should be told of the event but asked to state their special needs in order to cover the story. They may wish to make a preliminary visit, film on a different day or at a different time, or tape interviews prior to the press reception. Television teams may take hours to produce a few minutes worth of screen time. Moreover, both equipment and technicians have to be booked to cover the story. Or the PR officer himself may provide radio stations with taped interviews, using the services of news agencies.

ORGANIZING A PRESS CONFERENCE OR RECEPTION

The following considerations must be borne in mind when organizing these three kinds of press events.

The purpose

There must be a good reason for the conference or reception. Would a news release suffice? Is there a big enough story to warrant taking up the time of the media, let alone the expense to be incurred? Are you absolutely clear about what you want to tell and show the media?

The date

What is the best date? Many factors will control this choice — such as the purpose of the event and the availability of the venue. The correct choice of date is vital. For example, if a new central air conditioning system is to be introduced, the press reception should be held early in the year in order to achieve coverage in the pre-summer published A/C features. March is most preferable, April would be getting rather late.

To make sure that the right speaker is free, it may be necessary to work a long way out, and there is not much sense in holding an event on a day when preferred journalists are attending something else. It is by no means easy to avoid a clash of dates sometimes, but it does pay to be as thorough as possible. Many newspapers publish a weekly table of forthcoming activities and a guide to exhibitions being held at home and abroad during the current and following year. The time of day for a press gathering is much more important than is sometimes supposed. Businesspeople are inclined to think first of their own convenience and availability, and to regard these events as cocktail parties that commence at 7:00 P.M. — after office hours so as not to interfere with the day's work. But the guests have homes to go to. They do not all work on national newspapers whose offices are open day and night. They, too, like to keep office hours. It is no pleasure for them, and not really a duty, to have to forsake dinner at home with their families to attend an evening press event.

If the organizer does insist on an evening affair, he or she must expect to attract office juniors and freelance contributors to whom the invitations have been passed by more senior people who prefer to attend press functions held at more convenient times.

So, generally speaking, the best time for a press conference or reception is between 11:00 A.M. on a Monday or Tuesday (Wednesday is bad for journalists working on weeklies) during the first or last ten days of the month (mid-month is bad for journalists working on monthlies). Reporters should be given their stories before lunchtime, and an evening paper reporter will want his story as early in the day as possible. If the guests are likely to be inundated with invitations, a convenient venue allows them to attend more than one event during the same morning or afternoon. This is often true of women's magazines and women's page journalists who go from one reception to another.

The venue

A venue should be chosen because it suits the occasion, provides the correct facilities, is conveniently located, has the right appeal, and makes reasonable charges for exemplary catering. That is a short list of requirements, no more.

▶ Choosing the venues for PR events calls for knowledge of the advantages and disadvantages of a large variety of premises, and for this reason it pays to continuously put on file information about all eligible hotels, halls, and other accommodations. Careful selection is necessary and usually one finds that only a limited number of establishments are worth retaining on this recommended list.

▶ Many big hotels possess a magnificently appointed lecture hall that is ideal for conferences. Other problems, though, can prevent the use of otherwise attractive venues in some cities, e.g., lack of parking facilities.

In selecting a venue outside a city, the organizer has to cater to guests traveling in from other towns, usually by car.

Let us summarize the eight main considerations to be borne in mind when booking venues for press gatherings:

▶ Availability of a room or rooms of the required size, and whether this accommodation is also available earlier in the day or on the previous day for preparation or rehearsal purposes.

▶ Does the accommodation meet the special demands of the occasion? For instance, does it black out for films? Is it soundproof? Is the floor strong enough for weighty exhibits (ballroom floors seldom are)? Are there convenient coat room facilities, especially for raincoats and umbrellas on rainy days?

▶ Is the catering good? Are there any specialties?

▶ Is the venue or its location of special interest?

▶ What are the costs per head for finger buffets, lunches, and dinners? Is there a hire charge for rooms? What is the method and rate for gratuities? (Comparative costs are more important than one might think.)

▶ Has the venue special facilities such as lighting effects, staging microphones, projectors, video players, screens, tape recorders, and computer equipment? Some are extremely well equipped for PR events.

▶ Is there a parking garage or are the premises adjacent to one? Apart from guests' cars, space may be required for a demonstration vehicle.

▶ Are transportation facilities good, e.g., taxis and other forms of public transportation? And is the venue easily accessible at busy times of the day? Accessibility can have a critical effect on attendance figures if a number of PR events happen to be claiming the same people on the same day.

Other considerations may arise according to the needs of the occasion. A hotel or restaurant may be required to provide lunch for a press party visiting a factory or an installation. What is the capacity of the dining room? Or it might be an attraction to invite the press to a brand new hotel that has novelty appeal. It may be that outside caterers can be brought in to provide for a party in a historic venue, such as a museum.

Few venues are suitable for every event, and if press parties are being held in various parts of the country, satisfactory answers will be required to many questions. The important thing is knowing what questions to ask! It is not sufficient merely to write or telephone; venues should be inspected before making firm reservations.

So we have three major issues to resolve before anything further is decided: Is there a big enough story to warrant holding the event at all? When and where do we hold the function?

The invitation list

This should not be a big problem for the experienced press officer, and certainly not if the press officer is dealing most of the time with a limited, specialized press. It can be more difficult for the consultancy dealing with a much larger assortment of journals and journalists. The list should have not just the addresses of the journalists but individual names of the invitees.

To produce a reliable invitation list, it is necessary to do a lot of research because journalists change their jobs with remarkable frequency. In fact, it is true to say that if the same organization held a reception twice a year, there would be considerable changes in each succeeding invitation list.

Invitations, whether cards, letters, or emails, have to be made out to individuals as they are considered personal communications. They cannot be sent vaguely to unidentified persons. This may come as a surprise to those who run off grubby-looking invitation letters on copiers and send them in unsealed envelopes to unnamed editors. Not surprisingly, such invitations produce little or no response and the organizer fills the reception with company staff to make it appear as though there is good attendance. Good attendance is won by taking infinite pains.

When the company prepares an invitation list, it must be large enough to produce a satisfactory turnout. If the aim is to have an attendance of 40, it may be necessary to invite 60, perhaps more. Clearly, the attendance will depend upon various factors, including newsworthiness, attractiveness of venue, and convenience of place, date, and time. But in addition, there are other considerations, such as staff shortages in the office, personal illness, and holidays, which are beyond the control of the organizers and therefore deplete numbers even after acceptances have been received. On these occasions, the press officer must never be overoptimistic and it is foolish to boast to employer or client that this and that paper will be represented. Major newspapers tend to accept everything and then make their choice on the day of an event.

The invitations

The news may be so "hot" that a telephoned invitation will be justified, and this is possible when the invitation list is a small one. Or the list may be extremely specialized, and the press officer may personally know all the journalists so that the officer can invite them all by telephone at short notice. But these are exceptions to the usual run of PR events, possible with press conferences but unnecessary with press receptions, which have to be planned over a matter of weeks so that there is ample time in which to give journalists seven to ten days' notice, sometimes longer.

The timing of the dispatch of invitations is of importance to the overall organization of the event. There must be a date prior to the event when a reasonable knowledge of likely numbers is required so that catering, transport, seating, and other arrangements can be confirmed with banquet managers and contractors. This day may be three to seven days in advance of the actual date. And if, for some reason, capacity is limited, it may be necessary to stagger the dispatch of invitations in order to control the total number of acceptances, with further invitations being sent out to make up for refusals as they come in.

Out of courtesy to guests, the invitations must either be a well-produced letter or, better still, a printed invitation card. A card is always preferable, and letters should be resorted to only when there is no time to print a card or when numbers do not justify the design and print cost. A card has many advantages over a letter. It is a special piece of correspondence, arriving in an important-looking white envelope. Out of politeness it cannot be ignored. It does its job well. Invitation cards are often put on mantelpieces and window sills where other people see them. And if the design and printing is neat and distinctive, it will help to make the event seem worth attending. The inference is that if the host is prepared to go to some trouble to invite guests properly, the host will surely go to the same trouble to make sure that the event is worth attending.

There was a time when it was thought that invitation cards had to be given the copperplate look, but the vogue of script typefaces has now been superseded by the use of neat modern typefaces.

When designing cards, thought should be given to the way in which replies will be returned. The organizer needs to know the refusals as well as the acceptances, and the best way to obtain definite answers one way or the other is to provide an easy means of reply. When a means of reply is used, a fairly accurate idea of acceptances will be known within 48 hours, while knowledge of refusals provides opportunity for follow-ups or dispatch of fresh invitations. There are several ways of doing this: reply slips, reply cards, or addressed envelopes, but by far the best method is to incorporate an addressed reply card with the invitation card. The two cards offer four sides for printing. On the face of one card is the invitation. On the back of the invitation, a timetable program of the event should be set out. The reply card should repeat the basic details of the event and have space for the guest to indicate acceptance or refusal — "I can/I cannot" — and give his or her name and publication. The reverse side of the reply portion should bear the organizer's full postal address, and in the top right-hand corner a frame to indicate business-free reply postage or to request a response by mail.

The following is an example of simple, informative, and effective wording.

The Directors of XYZ Ltd.

have pleasure in inviting

---

to attend a **Press Reception**

in the **Crystal Room**

Plaza Hotel, New York

on **Tuesday, November 5th**

at **11:30 a.m.**

to view the new **XYZ Models for 200_.**

Cocktails
Refreshments

RSVP John Smith, XYZ Ltd.
Phone 123-456-7890
Fax 456-789-0123
johnsmith@emailaddy.com
One Fifth Avenue
New York, NY 10000

This card does require the organizer to neatly hand-write in the names of each guest. If there is a very large invitation list this handwriting may be too big a task and the alternative is to have a card that reads:

The Directors of XYZ Ltd. have pleasure in inviting you to attend a PRESS RECEPTION

The wording of the invitation should be clearly set to put all the facts that will encourage the recipient to decide to attend if he or she possibly can. A press reception has to be marketed like anything else, hence the attention to detail. This marketing attitude is vital because invitations must compete with many other claims upon a journalist's time, including rival invitations.

The invitation card should also indicate the kind of refreshments that will be provided, and the address for reply should be printed at the bottom of the invitation even though a reply card is attached or enclosed.

The appearance of the card will be enhanced if it carries the organization's coat of arms or the company logo, and it should comply with the accepted house style regarding typeface and color.

Should there be any sort of enclosure with an invitation card? The answer is yes, if it will do anything to encourage the journalist to attend. It may be a personal note, or if it is a complicated or controversial subject it may be a good idea to include some preliminary information that will stimulate curiosity and questions. But it can be fatal to send out the news release in advance.

A telephone or an email follow-up may be worthwhile. When telephoned, some people will say they have never seen the invitation, and this may be perfectly true. There may be other reasons why the prospective guest has not replied, and a few friendly words on the telephone may very likely encourage an acceptance. After all, one has to sell a press reception.

For the day of the event, a complete list of acceptances should be made up, and this can be checked against signatures in the visitors' book so that absentees may be sent the news releases and pictures they would have received had they attended.

Identifying guests

It has become accepted at receptions, meetings, and conferences that everyone should wear some form of identification. This practice has the distinct advantage of making contact and conversation much easier. By means of badges, preferably adhesive, which name both guest and publication, the press officer can move among guests, quickly scanning badges and welcoming people by name.

Members of the host party should wear badges of a different color, or that bear the organization's logo.

The badges should be prepared from the acceptance list, and set out in alphabetical order on the reception table at the entrance to the room where the reception is being held.

Press kits or packs

It is not advisable to hand out press kits as guests arrive as it is difficult to eat, drink, talk, and read at the same time. Packets can be available on the reception table for those who ask for information in advance. (Over-elaborate so-called kits are unnecessary for PR events and can be costly.) Often a simple news release is all that is needed with pictures and photographs numbered on a board and available for order. If press packets are absolutely necessary, the best are undoubtedly the pliable plastic ones that can even be rolled and put in a jacket pocket if need be. The simplest is the transparent kind, but there are more sophisticated ones with button-down flaps which are useful and more secure when material is being collected during a prolonged visit or tour.

Electronic press kits can be posted to an organization's web site after a press conference, reception or another event.

Catering

When giving numbers to the caterer, it is safe to work on a number slightly below that of the acceptance list, since not all of the guests remain for the buffet. While it is extremely embarrassing to have insufficient food, it is equally poor management and economics to have a lot of food left over. The bar can be controlled by one of two methods: the bartender can be given a maximum figure, at which point he or she asks the organizer whether the bar should remain open, or the bar can be closed at a certain time and coffee can be served thereafter.

The serving of coffee is an excellent device for bringing the proceeding to a close, and, since by coffee time numbers are sure to be depleted, it is almost certain to be sufficient to order only half as many coffees as the total number of people present. With proper management, press events can be budgeted and controlled in a sensible and responsible manner.

Food is more important than the bar. If a host really wants to impress the press, good food is by far the best method. The food should include some substantial items and not miniature sandwiches lost under a maze of mustard and lettuce. The organizer should insist on not only seeing a variety of menus and prices, but should clearly understand from the banquet manager what is meant by each item. It is not good management to accept a banquet manager's vague assurances that he can "do something for so much a head, sir." It is sometimes surprising how much better one can do for less when one demands that each item be detailed.

Gifts and mementos

Should the press be given gifts at a press reception? It depends on the suitability of the gift or memento to the subject of the reception. A gift is not vital, but if it is a product sample or is related in some way to the organization running the reception, it can be both appropriate and desirable. There are some organizations from which such gifts might well be expected, but otherwise gifts are more appropriate to facility visits where they are an accepted courtesy. A gift should not appear to be a bribe, but merely a nice gesture, and if it is a matter of proving one's case by providing a sample it will, of course, be a very good tactic.

There was the famous, or infamous, TV program when a motoring correspondent displayed an array of gifts he had received from manufacturers. One baby car manufacturer gave motoring correspondents a free car. On the other hand, the sewing machine company that presented 120 guests at a press reception with a child's toy sewing machine made a nice gesture. But a clock manufacturer, launching a new type of clock at a press reception, gave everyone a clock and was chagrined afterwards to receive complaints that the gift clocks did not work.

Managing the event

This chapter has stressed that a PR event must be planned right down to the last detail, and that there must be a properly planned program. The press officer has to be both producer and stage manager. People have to do certain things correctly at stipulated times, and a press reception is not just "played by ear." Only the press officer can coordinate and manage the various elements, and everyone from managing director to distinguished guest must comply with the press officer's control. A good press officer will operate almost invisibly, and the event will seem to run itself, but all the same, the press officer must be here, there, and everywhere making certain that everything proceeds on course.

By setting out the program on the invitation, the press officer commits everyone concerned to a timetable. Speeches must be prepared so that copies can be made available to the press; there must be a rehearsal, with or without the VIP speaker; and the press officer can chair the meeting, thereby making certain that the program runs to time.

One of the controlling factors will be the accessibility of the location. If more than one hotel exists by the same name, the location of the one selected must be clearly stated. If there is an indicator board in the foyer of the hotel, the organizer must check that the event is correctly listed and described. If there is any risk of guests losing their way along corridors, there should be directional notices. If the event occurs in the winter or on a wet day, coat checking should be clearly indicated. The reception table at the door should be adequately staffed to receive guests. The organizer should be present to welcome guests and do anything necessary to expedite their entry.

If the organization or the client has been made responsible for the supply of products or materials, the organizer must make sure that they have in fact arrived and are ready for use. The same applies to the arrival of computer equipment and screen.

The reception period will usually run for 20 to 30 minutes, the shorter the better. During this period, refreshments will be served according to the time of day, and guests will be introduced to members of the host party. The reception period must not drag and will continue only so long as a reasonable number of guests have yet to arrive. If the reception portion goes on too long, the press will become restless and want to know when the program is to begin. The organizer must therefore judge the atmosphere of the assembly and be aware of the attendance building up. The organizer must judge the right moment to proceed to the next item on the program, being careful to keep to the time schedule.

Throughout the course of the event, the press officer must make sure that the timetable is adhered to — the showing of the film, the speech-giving, any demonstrations, and finally the invitation to enjoy refreshments and ask questions of the host party. During this latter period, the organizer will endeavor to meet as many of the guests as possible and see that they are satisfied with answers to their questions and are supplied with accurate information. The press officer should also endeavor to say goodbye to each guest on departing and thank them for attending.

Finally, the press officer will have to pay the account for the hotel's services and offer his or her feedback on the way in which the hotel contributed to the event's success. This will establish good relations which can be invaluable for the future.

Gimmicks are apt to have boomerang effects, and journalists are quick to deride attempts to invent stories. On the other hand, if the product is somewhat mundane a little originality can succeed. There is the example of Knorr in Zurich who invited the press to review two new products, two-portion soups and gravy in a tube. The Knorr invitation read (this is a translated version of the original German message):

> *As new styles of living develop, our eating habits change and this leads to a constant flow of new requirements being made of the food products industry. It is the task of a modern concern in this sector to recognize and meet these new requirements. In this connection, the Knorr Food Products Co. Ltd. has created two new products and is happy to have the opportunity of presenting these to you at the press information lunch. Let us surprise you at the premiere!*

The reception took place between 11.30 A.M. and 2 P.M. at the Koch-Studio, Zurich. The focal point was a performance by two artists, well known in Switzerland. On the basis of information supplied from Knorr, these artists wrote two skits in which the new products were highlighted. In this entertaining fashion the press were told about the soups and gravy in a tube. In addition, more fun was added to the occasion by giving the journalists a hobby cook's apron (designed by a cartoonist) which bore the words, "I feel so soupy." The apron had five pockets at the lower edge to hold samples of the five new Knorr soup varieties. There was also an on-the-scene contest while journalists were sampling the soups — they had to write down whatever came into their heads as they tasted the soups, and prizes were awarded for the most original comments.

Eighty Swiss newspapers and magazines reported on the new products, some in the form of articles illustrated with pictures of the artists during their performance.

Organizing a facility visit

While most of the items already discussed about press conferences and receptions will also apply to the preparation of a facility visit, there are several additional items to consider.

This category of facility visit includes all those visits by parties of journalists to factories, installations, sites, etc., which require conveyance of guests, or at least the management of guests at some distant or outside location, as distinguished from receiving them in the head office boardroom or in a hotel in the vicinity of publishing offices. It also includes trips on new trains, ships, or aircraft, provided by the owners to the press to gain first-hand knowledge and experience. It can involve no more than a single journalist who is being given facility to write an article, or a party of almost any size. Such visits can be very complicated planning feats calling for patient preparation over a long period. Journalists are unwilling or unable to give up a day, perhaps two days, on a facility visit unless there is real justification. Complaints are made from time to time about wonderfully arranged charter plane trips with generous hospitality and souvenir gifts, but no story!

As we said when considering the press reception, there must be a clear and valid purpose for any PR event, but particularly so for one that will occupy so much of a journalist's time. It must add to his or her knowledge and experience, supply background materials, show promise of future news development, or give an immediate story. It must be of value to journalists in their daily work. They must go home feeling glad that they accepted the invitation, and not feeling that it was all very nice but rather a waste of time. Some well-known organizations spend many thousands of dollars to achieve no more than that. These ill-conceived jaunts do the PR business no good at all.

Let us analyze the practical requirements of facility visits.

PARTY NUMBERS

The primary consideration when planning a press visit is the number of people in the proposed party.

CAPACITY OF THE PREMISES

Visitors to a factory can be a nuisance to those working there, but this must never be apparent! A certain number of people can be handled comfortably, whether it be inside a laboratory or factory or at an outdoor site. No more than 15 people might be acceptable in a research establishment, whereas six parties of 15 might be all right in a large factory.

On most factory visits small groups need to be arranged because production operations would be lost on a crowd, and so the usual practice is to organize parties of six to 12 people, each with a guide. This may therefore decide how many groups can be taken round in the available time between arrival and lunchtime, or in the afternoon before the party must leave. One method of overcoming the time problem is to let these groups follow different routes, rather than have them following one behind the other. In this way, all groups can complete their tours at very nearly the same time, and visitors are not left hanging about waiting for the others to catch up with them.

This clearly calls for some good planning and rehearsal. Guides must know what they are talking about and be capable of answering questions, yet all take about the same time in dealing with each section of the tour. There should be a manual for the guides to study, and rehearsal should include practice tours that are carefully timed and observed by the organizer. It is no use detailing members of the staff for guide duties and then just hoping for the best on the actual tour visit day.

CATERING AND ACCOMMODATION

Party numbers may be controlled by the seating capacity of the dining room at the factory, or at a local hotel or restaurant. If there is suitable outdoor space a tent may be the answer. Again, if a large party is desirable, seating limitations can be overcome by having a buffet with a minimum number of tables, although a party which has been tramping around a factory will prefer an opportunity to sit down and relax at lunchtime. But these are the sorts of alternatives that need to be thought about carefully.

Naturally, it is more pleasant to keep a party together if an overnight stay is necessary, and a member of the host party should stay at the hotel with the guests. Local conditions may demand scattering the party among different hotels, but this should be avoided if possible. Many members of the press party will know one another and will enjoy the opportunity of staying in the same hotel. If a party does have to be split up, it is a good idea to find out if any of the guests do wish to stay together, and accommodations should be organized to meet individual wishes, whenever possible.

Attention to small personal details can be most important to the success of an event. If block bookings have been made, the actual assignment of rooms at different hotels can be given during the coach, train, or plane journey. To do this well a team of organizers is required with hosts, couriers, or guides attached to each grouping of guests. The guests must never be left unattended, never expected to move from **A** to **B** unescorted once they have someone detailed with a car to pick up latecomers or stragglers so that there is no danger of anyone failing to join the party.

A point worth remembering in this respect is that if guests have to travel a long distance to join the transportation (as when airports are some distance from city centers), it is safer to collect people in a central place and provide transportation to the airport. It is comparatively simple for guests to assemble at a suitable well-known spot that is accessible by most forms of transportation. Bus companies can usually advise on the best meeting places because they have pick-up points agreed upon between them and the police. Some airports are conveniently served by rail services so that transportation is easily arranged and controlled.

CAPACITY OF TRANSPORTATION

Numbers may be determined by the peculiarities of the seating capacity, the party booking arrangements, or the mode of transportation. If a bus has 42 seats it is obviously impossible to accept 43 guests. The same limitation applies to airplanes. It is not always possible to charter a larger bus or airplane. Trains are more flexible to a point, but the organizer must discuss with railway staff the make-up of the train and the kind of stock being used since this differs considerably according to the region. It is essential to know how the seating will be dispersed, and it may be desirable to restrict the party to a single coach. Alternatively, the minimum size of the party could be the total seating of an entire coach.

When chartering airplanes, there may be a choice of aircraft and this selection will again depend on members. Similarly, if seats are being reserved on a scheduled passenger service there may be an advantage in a number that secures a price reduction. These points should be discussed at the earliest possible time with the airline.

The commercial staff of transportation operators can be exceedingly helpful, but it is wise to check everything and not rely too heavily on other people to take over one's responsibilities. On one occasion it was discovered at very short notice that railway tickets had been incorrectly dated, which would have invalidated them when presented to the ticket collector on the train. Fortunately, the wrong date was discovered in good time; otherwise, the press visit might have been a disaster. Tickets should not be posted to guests; it is safer to ask guests to exchange a voucher for a ticket supplied by the organizer at the place of departure.

An important lesson can be learned from the last statement: an organizer must be a born pessimist. The organizer must literally try to think of everything that could possibly go wrong so that he or she can then find a satisfactory solution to it. For example, in a certain town, the police insisted that buses must unload at a distance from the hotel. This could have meant some of the party losing their way. So the organizer argued and the police relented, permitting the buses to unload outside the hotel itself and returning at an agreed-upon time, which meant that the activities within the venue had to run strictly to time. But this sort of thing can be done only if the organizer has a sufficiently nimble mind to foresee trouble.

LIMITED INVITATION LIST

When the topic is so specialized that there is a limited invitation list, the problem is to find a date when the majority can attend. This difficulty is best overcome by offering alternative dates by telephone, then negotiating in this way until a sufficiently large party has been assembled. When this practice is followed, the visit will hinge on the date most acceptable by the guests.

THE BUDGET

It may be physically possible to accommodate and transport a hundred people but the cost may be prohibitive. Whatever facilities or limitations may exist, it is essential to have the event strictly costed and to work within an agreed-upon cost range. Every expense can be known in advance and nothing should be agreed upon without a prior quotation. "Shopping list" budgets for press events are outlined in the previous chapter.

INVITATIONS

For this type of operation, the invitation must give specific details about the object of the visit and the facilities for transportation and accommodations that will be provided, accompanied by a timetable from start to finish, including the picking up and returning of guests. Depending upon how complicated the arrangements may be, an invitation ticket as already described for press receptions may be adequate or it may be safer to include a cover letter setting out the itinerary.

Because so many reservations have to be finalized once numbers are known, it is necessary to dispatch invitations much earlier than in the case of press receptions. Travel agents, bus companies, and caterers will want a week's notice of the final arrangements, so if time is required for sending out a second round of invitations should initial acceptance numbers be unsatisfactory, the original invitation will need to go out a month before the date of the event. This means that copy must go to the printer at least two weeks before delivery is required, and time must also be allowed to either side of the printing dates for the finalization of details and the design of the card and then, when delivered, the making out and mailing of the cards.

Thus, at least two months in advance of the event, we must know exactly what is going to happen. Working backwards yet again, it is not going to be too soon to begin making plans three months in advance, and no doubt some thought will have been given to the idea of a press visit much earlier than that.

It is important to see that the right people join the party. Such an expensive event merits the attendance of senior editorial personnel — it is not just a day out for juniors, freeloaders, and hangers-on. Pointing out that numbers are restricted and that it will be a privilege to attend will emphasize this. It does happen sometimes that when a very attractive press visit is learned about, a number of journalists will phone and ask to be invited. And some who were not invited will call and complain about this afterwards. This only goes to illustrate another of the pitfalls of media relations — you can be too successful!

PARTY BRIEFING

No matter what details may have been sent at the time of the invitation's dispatch, each person who has accepted must be sent detailed instructions three to seven days prior to the event. The instructions should not be sent too soon or they may be mislaid; they should not be sent too late or they may be delayed in the mail or in the publishing house's internal postal system. Before leaving home, every guest should know exact details of the program of the visit.

It is unwise to issue assembly instructions in advance, and then to issue the rest of the instructions during the journey or upon arrival, although it is sensible to reissue instructions in case anyone has left them behind. Knowledge of the scheme of things will enable people to bring suitable clothing, accessories, and equipment that might include such things as raincoats, sunglasses, cameras, or field glasses. A thoughtful organizer ensures successful events.

Some organizers hand out elaborate press kits as soon as they greet guests — when these kits are clumsy cardboard wallets, it really is a problem to know what to do with them. A sheet of paper that can go into a pocket or handbag is much better appreciated.

NEWS STORY FACILITIES

If journalists are likely to need working facilities so that they can get stories, pictures, tapes, or film back to their offices in time for release that day, facilities must not only be provided but also made known in advance. Telephones, computers, lighting facilities, and transportation may be necessary. It is useless inviting people to cover a story that they cannot communicate to their editors in good time for publication or broadcast.

TIMING

The organizer must time events, such as VIP visits and official openings, so that they occur before lunch and there is time to communicate the story to evening papers, the internet, and radio and TV news services, which are typically broadcast from 5:00 P.M. on. This timing of press visits will be controlled by the location of the venue, and also by whether the party is staying overnight or traveling to and from the venue during the day.

Day return visits present problems that require very tight and foolproof schedules, and much will depend upon the speed of the transportation. We must accept that the earliest a party may be able to leave a city center — to which members have already traveled from their homes — is 9:00 A.M. and it should be back by 5:30 P.M. since some members of the party may well have to undertake a considerable additional journey to reach their homes. Add to this the fact that many factories close for lunch and close for the day at a specific time and there are very strict time limitations within which a visit has to be planned.

Every item in the program must therefore be timed — this means rehearsing and timing every movement of the party, making special allowances for the time it takes for a given number of people to leave or enter a vehicle or building, cross roads, ascend stairs, or attend demonstrations. An experienced press officer can estimate these times without having to resort to a mock rehearsal, but it does pay to go over the sequence of movements where they will actually happen. Even then it is wise to insert in the timetable some extra minutes so that the program is flexible enough to allow for losses of time through lateness of any transportation, unexpected weather conditions, or some other minor setback on the day.

This programming should be so expertly done that the party proceeds comfortably throughout the sequence of events without anyone being conscious of being "organized" and only that everything runs smoothly.

Although a program may be carefully planned and scrupulously rehearsed, it seldom actually goes like clockwork because trains can run late, aircraft are notorious for being late, traffic does get held up, people get lost, and something always takes longer than expected. But this does not matter if the organizer has taken the unexpected into account.

As an example, the timetable for a women's press party to a town permitted various delays in transportation in the event there was time to spare and the coach took a detour along the scenic coast. It was a day of constant adaptation as there were a number of substitutes in the party, which meant a change in the table plan, and one member missed the train but joined the party later. However, a story was written afterwards congratulating the organizer on a visit that ran like clockwork.

But it may not be necessary, possible, or advisable to take a press party to a distant location with all its costs and inherent troubles of transporting, feeding, and accommodating perhaps a hundred people over a period of, say, 36 hours. The event could be televised, conveyed by mail, websites, landline, and shown on a giant screen to a press audience in a hotel. Hiring the landline or satellite is expensive, but the total operation is simpler and can be economical if it is a big story capable of earning substantial coverage.

CHAPTER 8

Corporate Financial Public Relations

WHAT IS FINANCIAL PUBLIC RELATIONS?

When it comes to a single company's financial relations, the investing public can be divided into two categories: (1) actual shareholders of publicly-owned corporations, and (2) professional financial opinion leaders. In the first group, many owners of securities are new investors seeking a better return on accumulated savings; many are novices in financial affairs, unfamiliar with the specialized language of the financial community. The second group consists of the security analysts, mutual fund researchers, and managers like Fidelity Mutual Funds, investment counselors, insurance company analysts and executives, bank officers, stock and share brokers who influence the judgment of other investors.

Benefits from good financial public relations

The growth of financial public relations can be traced to many factors. Among them are the need for equity financing arising out of the tremendous post-war growth, educational campaigns by the stock exchanges to encourage investment in publicly-owned corporations, and the existence of a broad group of individuals looking for ways to put their money to work.

Financial PR is not a means to "push up" the price of a company's securities. While informed stockholders and professional analysts may indeed help to maintain a better stock price, good financial public relations can increase the ability to borrow funds, attract and hold key personnel, lead to more favorable terms when arranging corporate loans, or issuing stock.

Besides circulating information on a company's position in its industry, its current activities, earnings, and future prospects so it can be evaluated as an investment, a program of financial PR leads to a broader base of stock ownership, a stronger bargaining position when acquisitions are made through the exchange of stock, and support from stockholders and the financial community during a period of adversity.

Shareholders can often become customers too, or at least sales people of goodwill for the company. Articulate, loyal shareholders work in a company's interest buying its products and urging others to do so.

How to communicate with shareholders

Few active investors have the time or knowledge to analyze the comparative merits of securities. Some rely on what they read in journals devoted to commercial intelligence, market letters, or stock brokerage releases; some depend on recommendations from their investment advisers, bankers, brokers, security analysts, and trustees of estates; some weigh the information in annual reports.

A corporation must prepare an audited financial statement for its stockholders once a year and must prepare quarterly financial statements. But in today's competitive money markets it is rare that a company stops at the legal minimum. Most companies use personal visits, telephone calls, mailings, and supplementary reports to keep shareholders informed, interested, and satisfied.

Some companies put their annual reports on the internet for the stockholders, the press, suppliers, and selected persons in the financial community; and each new stockholder receives a personal welcoming letter encouraging him or her to ask questions anytime. Some companies send out reprints of speeches and magazine articles by company officials, copies of the company's internal or external house publications, special fact books containing statistical information on the headquarters country as well as brochures on the company. Companies often arrange for interviews and plant visits by interested analysts.

HOW DOES THE INVESTING PUBLIC CHOOSE THE RIGHT COMPANY TO INVEST IN?

▶ Take a good look at the profit and loss statement.

▶ Study the balance sheet carefully.

▶ Consider the intrinsic value of the shares.

▶ Find out from the experience of existing shareholders.

▶ Judge the standing of the company in the industry it is in.

▶ Assess the company's contribution to the community.

WHAT THE UNIONS NEED TO KNOW

The annual report of an enterprise is a rich source of information on two key issues that concern employees — that of pay and job security.

On the pay issue, most major corporations throughout the world report on:

▶ the average number of employees by category of activity and location, and

▶ operating costs including employment costs classified in categories of wage and salary costs, social security costs, and other pension costs

Armed with this information, workers' representatives can calculate:

▶ the average pay per employee

▶ movements in the real purchasing power of their members, by adjusting changes in average pay using the index of consumer (or retail prices), and

▶ the share of net corporate income that has been paid to the employee

These calculations become even more useful if the negotiator can obtain the corporate reports for earlier years, from which trends can be identified.

On the issue of job security, the annual report and financial statements will contain a wealth of information that should enable workers' representatives to come to an informed view on how the company is doing in the marketplace.

In particular, the report can contain details of:

▶ the growth or decline in the labor force by location and activity

▶ changes in sales costs and profitability — is the company being run efficiently?

▶ the level of capital expenditure — is the company investing in the future?

➤ changes in the financial structure — is the company financially stable? Is it financing operations by heavy borrowing? Are there adequate reserves of working capital to cover current expenditure and short-term liabilities?

Many of these indicators of financial efficacy can be assessed, over a number of years, by the calculation of ratios, and a whole series of ratios can then be inserted in a model for economic and financial analysis.

The CEO's report

The main function of the chief executive officer's portion of the annual report is to provide information about the enterprise's activities, its directors, its labor force, the structure of ownership, and details of any donations given to charities or political organizations.

The balance sheet

The balance sheet is another statement that all corporations must prepare at the end of the financial year and make available for public inspections. The primary purposes of the balance sheet are:

➤ to indicate the net worth of the company at the time the balance sheet was drawn up

➤ to indicate the nature of the assets held and to show how the acquisition of these assets was paid for

➤ to show the relative values of short-term and long-term assets and liabilities

How have these assets been acquired? Usually in a number of ways, including borrowing, selling shares, or running down accumulated cash reserves. This process places an obligation on the enterprise to repay its creditors, pay dividends to the shareholders when possible, or rebuild the reserves. In other words, they are liabilities. In more detail, these liabilities comprise short-term (current) commitments such as suppliers' unpaid bills, current loan repayments, and overdrafts; and long-term liabilities such as loans, income raised through the issue of shares, and reserves accumulated from profits and reevaluations in the past.

To summarize, a balance sheet should contain the following main headings:

ASSETS

➤ Fixed assets

▶ Intangible assets (R&D, patents, trademarks, goodwill, payment on account)

▶ Tangible assets (machinery, buildings, vehicles, etc.)

▶ Financial assets (part ownership of other companies' pension funds, long-term loans to other companies, etc.)

▶ Current assets (cash, accounts receivables, inventory, prepayments)

LIABILITIES

▶ Current liabilities (short-term creditors, overdrafts, etc.)

▶ Capital employed (total assets minus current liabilities), represented by long-term loans and other long-term creditors, share capital, and accumulated reserves

▶ Total capital and reserves (equals capital employed)

Chapter 9

Community Service

ORIGIN

The origin of the word *community* reflects its spirit. It comes from the Latin word *communis* which is composed of "com," meaning together, and "munis" meaning ready to be of service. "Ready to be of service together" — that implies not only being in the same boat, but pulling (together) in unison on the oars. The community is the heart of any service organization. It draws its strength from the willingness on the part of the service organization members to work together towards commonly agreed-upon goals. A service organization, such as Rotary, Lions, Kiwanis, and Soroptimists — may have lawyers, teachers, physicians, merchants, and other professions represented.

As a member of such service organizations:

▶ the lawyer's profession is to enforce justice in it

▶ the teacher, to show light in it

▶ the physician, to keep it in health

▶ the merchant, to provide for it

All the members of the service organizations, each according to the profession he or she practices, can help people; there is a crying need for them — their talents, their training, and their concerns. They can inspire lay people to make valuable contributions to the community at large; they can make them priceless to the community.

The idea of community relations is as old as organized society. Ancient city states, such as Athens, existed on the strength of good relations with the citizens. In the Middle Ages, the powerful guilds set the pattern of charity and education in the towns.

COMMUNITY SERVICE OPERATION

Community service organizations have played a significant role in the development of social welfare the world over. Their distinguishing features are their capacity to enlist the cooperation of devoted workers, their ability to find material resources, their timely tackling of aggravating local needs and problems, and their willingness to experiment in different areas of community welfare. They are able to bring together a band of workers whose initiative and drive have not been thwarted by any outside interference. Thus, they enjoy a reasonable measure of administrative freedom in the planning of community services and this in itself is of considerable advantage in fostering a flexible approach in meeting emerging needs.

What makes a good community?

▶ Leaders who see the whole community
▶ A collective way of solving problems
▶ A strong sense of community loyalty
▶ A basically stable economy
These will help us considerably in understanding what makes a good community.

How communities show differences

Before launching on a program of civic improvement, we ought to understand the particular social traits of the people of the community. We ought to find answers to these questions:

▶ In what type of leader do our neighbors place more confidence?
▶ How are the people already organized to do the things they want done? That is, what is their social organization?
▶ How important to the citizens is the social ranking they give each other?
▶ What methods do they use to make individuals conform to accepted standards of thought and behavior?
▶ What do the people of our community consider most important in life? Or what are their social values?

How to promote a civic program

From the moment someone gets an idea to the completion of a project resulting from that idea, a program goes through five definite stages:

▶ Developing the idea

▶ Getting the facts

▶ Planning a program

▶ Launching the program

▶ Keeping up with the program

QUINTESSENCE OF CORPORATE PUBLIC RELATIONS

Attributes of strong corporate reputation

▶ Product quality

▶ Areas of perceived competence

▶ Leadership

▶ Technology

▶ Size

▶ Service

▶ Social responsibility

The attributes of an ideal corporate leader

To earn the reputation of an ideal leader of a business corporation, one should set an example by establishing:

▶ that the company/companies, which he or she presides over, can be both value driven and market driven

▶ that profits do not somehow preclude ethical behavior

▶ that growth is possible even if political patronage is not used to bend rules and cut corners

▶ that the pursuit of wealth can be, quite simply, graceful, and a mannerly one

▶ that he or she should, above all, personify the fact that businesspeople can succeed in conditions that are not ideal without lying or misrepresenting what is offered

Ten objectives of the corporate sector

▶ To raise the image of the company among its public

▶ To position the company's place of business and prestige competitively

▶ To safeguard the image, interests, and goodwill against the techniques of competitors

▶ To safeguard the interests of the shareholders and to place before the government views of the industry regarding trade, commerce and public policy concerns

▶ To explain to the investing public the future plans, programs, and prospects of the company's business activities

▶ To maintain law and order, peace and tranquility among staff personnel, workers, and labor unions by keeping them in close touch with the objectives of the corporate management

▶ To create better understanding among the community to assist in social reforms and discharge such other social responsibility(ies) towards the society or communities with which the organization is concerned or situated around

▶ To create "product and/or service image" among the consumers or end users

▶ To disseminate information concerning the company's activities, its objectives, its program for the future, its social program, etc., to the concerned public

▶ To achieve the objective of corporate success for growth and development in the future

These are the major objectives common to all types of organizations in corporate or non-corporate sectors. One needs to devote more attention and perception to each item.

Ten laws of corporate public relations planning

▶ Anything that can be changed will be changed until there is no time left for changing.

▶ Everything takes longer than you think.

▶ Every solution sometimes breeds new problems.

▶ It is impossible to make anything foolproof because fools are ingenious.

▶ There is no job so simple that it cannot be done wrong.

- Given a bad start, trouble will increase at an exponential rate.
- Almost anything is easier to get into than out of.
- Urgency varies inversely with importance.
- As you commence carrying out your plans, do not expect everything will come out successfully at each stage.
- No real problem has an easy solution.

How a company can stay close to the public

THE KEY

- Customers are first, employees second, shareholders third, and the community fourth.
- Think of yourself as the customer.
- Make every employee part of your vision.
- Monitor service internally to see that employees treat one another like customers.
- Listen to everyone who has a suggestion to offer.
- Prune bureaucracy so that everyone, notably the customer, can talk to you.
- The sales department is the lifeblood of any company; encourage the staff to stay in touch after the sale of your product or services.

Key to ideal corporate citizenship

ADHERING TO FAIRNESS

By this, it is meant that we must be fair to all the people with whom we have business relationships. These people are the consumers of our products or services and to whom we must be fair with regard to service, quality, and prices. We must be fair to our shareholders by ensuring that we generate a fair return on their investment. We must be fair to our employees in terms of compensation and benefits, and we must have a fair deal with other business associates. For example, we must not take undue advantage of our suppliers.

DEDICATION OF EXCELLENCE

. . . which means that we must always to do all our work in an efficient way. This is very important, particularly in today's environment where there are rapid technological changes and all kinds of crises and problems surrounding and affecting us. So we must make full use of our physical and intellectual efforts, knowledge, and skill to keep doing a better job all the time.

BELIEF IN THE VALUE OF THE INDIVIDUAL

This aspect has already been touched upon in the answer to the first point — **Adhering to Fairness**. However, we have to stress that our employees need to be considered as valuable assets. We start out with a good selection process to ensure that we make as few mistakes as possible. Then we attempt to treat them well in pay and fringe benefits — in short, take good care of them to get trained and developed in order to become true assets of the company. In return for treating our employees well, the organization receives loyalty and dedication.

CONCERN FOR SOCIAL RESPONSIBILITY

. . . which means be a good corporate citizen. We must want our company to place the national interest above commercial benefits. We do not pursue solely our profit objectives but conduct our business in a manner that reflects social responsibility. This approach is good for profitability.

In order to conduct business based on the beliefs discussed so far, the company must have business ethics. For the company to fulfill its business ethics, the employees must observe some do's and don'ts that we call a "code of conduct."

WHO ARE INTERESTED IN CORPORATE DISCLOSURES?

Any business unit has a number of stakeholders interested in knowing its performance results. They can be classified as:

▶ Shareholders (owners)

▶ Workers and employees

▶ Consumers

▶ Creditors

▶ Suppliers

▶ Society at large

Traditionally, it is only the owner or shareholder that has been considered the real stakeholder. This is no longer so because there are other parties who are equally interested in the health of the business and have an equally vital stake. The government, financial institutions not excluding securities markets, and financial analysts, are also watching the progress and growth of the business. In fact, performance of a business unit is not the achievement of the contributors of capital only. Many others also have contributed labor or service. As such, performance has to be taken note of and appraised by various stakeholders.

Corporate loyalty

The loyalty of people to other people, institutions, and ideals has always been crucial to the conduct of an orderly society. Good public relations can help employees understand the value of their company.

▶ In the context of relations between labor and management, it is not easy for companies to motivate employees to identify with corporate goals because the employees often do not have genuine feelings of attachment to the employer. Many employees tend to shy away from lasting attachments and regard their most intimate ties as being subject to severance, owing to closure of companies, arising from lack of broad-based policy of operation, layoffs in some cases, or retrenchment, and the like.

▶ Traditional concepts of loyalty will not survive. Loyalty — like business itself — will change, adhering to leaders whose actions command respect and commitment.

▶ In a corporate world that softens every blow with positive rhetoric about employees being members of the (corporate) family, both the employer and the employee may sometimes feel failure and guilt when the need arises to make decisions in the corporate interest.

▶ If corporate loyalty has to be redefined to contend with new facts of life, it must be done from the employee's point of view, not that of an employer who expects heroic efforts from people in return for a pay package that might not be forthcoming in the near future. It may seem a difficult task to elicit dedicated efforts from people whose futures are insecure, but the fact is that they basically want to think well of the company they work for, because it means thinking well of themselves, their friends, and colleagues. They will recognize the need for retrenchment, technological changes, and bigger individual workloads as long as it is honestly explained to them.

CHAPTER 10

Public Relations in a Crisis Situation

Crisis calls for management skills in prevention, preparation, and provision. Crises reduce the time span available to think effectively. Decisions have to be guided by rational thinking even under stress. Therefore, one has to come out with preplanned and immediate responses that diffuse the initial shock of a crisis.

Experts have noted that certain common features generally mark a crisis:

▶ The crisis may be unexpected and bewildering in dimension.

▶ The magnitude of the disaster — as in an explosion in a chemical plant killing many workers — may attract national and perhaps international attention.

▶ As stress increases, performance is likely to worsen. The possibility of inadequate performance is in direct proportion to the complexity of the task.

▶ The media will descend on the scene in no time. They will expect immediate answers to questions which one may not be able to answer at the time.

▶ In a crisis, communication may be open to conflicting interpretation.

▶ As many incidents have shown, one may have to deal with politics as well. Instead of being helpful, a section of politicians and government officials may be interested in promoting their own narrow interests. Planning for all these contingencies should be worked out at some quiet time before a crisis strikes.

Prevention, it is true, is better than cure. But very few crises can be foreseen. Yet the strange thing about the unforeseen is that it is always happening. A good manager, therefore, expects the unexpected and plans for it. Crisis management is taking instant control of the situation as soon as things have gone wrong. If the company does not take charge of a crisis, assuredly the crisis will take charge of the company, with the media dictating the agenda and setting the pace.

Readiness to deal with a crisis long before it occurs is the only rational approach. It also demonstrates the competence and confidence of the company to handle a crisis. The first impression is important because in the first 24 hours the company will be judged guilty until it is able to prove itself innocent. Indeed, crisis management is all about seizing initiative.

Planning can identify possible areas with potential for crisis. It may even reduce the possibility of a crisis and would at least control its magnitude. It can also certainly save reputations and avoid financial loss. Indeed, many companies today have well-oiled crisis management systems that slide into operation immediately if an accident or other crisis occurs.

Industrial disaster management has two aspects. While the *onsite* emergency plan deals with organizational setup, identifying who is in charge, and so forth, the *offsite* plan deals with the role of police, hospitals, and fire departments.

The key to crisis management lies in accomplishing several basic objectives:

▶ reducing psychological stress
▶ controlling panic
▶ responding to the emergency without delay
▶ mobilizing the necessary resources
▶ establishing communication channels
▶ ensuring high motivation and morale
▶ eliciting the participation of the media and the public

It is impossible to make any foolproof planning against the unforeseen. But even an awareness about the possibility of an unexpected development can generate considerable confidence and command, the two most vital attributes in tackling a crisis. The best way for negotiating crisis is to mobilize a well-rehearsed crisis management team, armed with an operational plan.

The team calls for expertise in all key areas, from legal to financial, personnel to sales, production to marketing.

Taking into consideration two or three imaginary but probable situations, a crisis plan identifies departmental and individual roles and responsibilities. Some may be specially subjected to surprise interviews to judge their reactions and reflexes. A key tool in a crisis plan is a clear step-by-step guideline for employees. It may include everything from prewritten press releases with gaps to be filled in to indicating where key officials may be available during the crisis. Simulated exercises may be conducted to test the efficacy of the plan.

All employees in the crisis prone area must be trained to follow a proper line of communication for reporting during a crisis. Some companies even designate crisis officers within all departments. In case of a crisis involving operational disaster, coordination with the nearby hospitals is essential. The relatives of the affected employees should be informed first before the information comes out in the media.

Clearly, the magnitude of a crisis will determine how best it can be contained. For some companies, deft handling of the crisis can convert a potential disaster into a triumph for the company, further enhancing their public credibility and confidence. History has shown only those who could evolve an effective crisis management program have survived to tell their tale.

Response to media

A major emergency can attract massive and instant interest from national and, possibly, international news media. Once an incident has occurred, the responsibility for informing the people through the media rests squarely on the shoulders of the company concerned. It will be the job of public relations officials to formulate and coordinate the company's media relations program in an emergency. It is quite likely that the media may get to know of the disaster before the company emergency procedures are fully set up. The reporters make regular calls to services like police, firefighters, and local hospitals. They might first come to know of the disaster from such sources. Immediately after the media become aware of a crisis, there can be a surge of telephone calls, quite possibly 24 hours a day for several days. This sheer speed can be one of the first problems.

The real danger of emergency media relations — of different sources giving incomplete or contradictory information — is present almost immediately. An information center may be operated around the clock. Some individuals may be specially trained to handle these telephone calls. To be fully effective, public information must be the specific responsibility of a senior executive with direct access to the CEO in an emergency situation. There should be a single source (spokesperson) to deal with the media to ensure consistent, accurate, precise, and timely information. He or she should be articulate, knowledgeable, and have an awareness of media deadlines. Speculation, gossip, and rumor fill the vacuum caused by failure to communicate during a crisis.

The decision as to whether a press statement should be issued or one will merely wait and reply to inquiries as and when they come has to be made without any delay. If a statement is issued, one must be very careful that the timing is very right. Telling the press something before telling the employees is not recommended. When a statement is read to a journalist over the phone, the journalist must be requested to read back to check that it is correct. All inquires should be channeled to the designated "press officer." It is vital that the press officer sticks exactly to the agreed-to statement and is not led to answer other questions. If the press officer is going to be interviewed, it is better to have a role-play rehearsal first with a colleague playing the part of the journalist.

The kind of questions usually asked in an emergency include:

▶ When did the emergency arise?
▶ Are there people dead/injured?
▶ How many?
▶ Where are they?
▶ Are people trapped?
▶ Is there a list of casualties?
▶ Have people been evacuated?
▶ Where to?
▶ Are there lists of names?
▶ Are there special telephone numbers or email addresses?
▶ What safeguards are there on the trains/aircraft involved?
▶ Who oversees them?
▶ How many policemen are at the scene?
▶ What problems are there?
▶ What are the effects on traffic?
▶ Emergency feeding/water/shelter/hospitals?

There can, of course, be many more questions, as well as requests for radio and TV interviews with those in charge and those at the scene of the disaster.

Both telephone inquiries and reporters on the spot need to be attended to with equal speed and effectiveness. If the disaster has an international dimension, such as an air crash involving foreign nationals, one will quite likely receive round-the-clock inquiries and requests for interviews from overseas media.

While developing a crisis management plan, training of senior managers in dealing with the media must be considered. The scale and nature of the emergency may require support from a number of people. It is important that the officers are selected by degree of sensitivity and consideration for time pressure of their normal work. Their constant availability to the media is essential. It is also important to provide the reporters with facilities like interview rooms, telecommunications services, and refreshments.

Shattered by the magnitude of a disaster, some companies seek to keep it out of public view by playing it down. The news about the crisis that is released to the media is often partial and delayed while the unfavorable facts are suppressed. But when these facts are ultimately made known — as they usually are, through insider leaks and government inquiries — the dishonest efforts to "cover up" the disaster land such companies into a further mess.

Years ago, in the airline industry, crisis planning meant that "one of the PR officer's first responsibilities when a crash occurred was to paint over the company's name on the wreckage before news photographers arrived." The prevalent strategy was to say as little as possible and keep the company's name out of the paper. Fortunately, times have changed.

Negative responses also have a significant impact on the employees. Seeing their company openly criticized through the nation's media causes confusion and demotivation. When all communication is directed at fighting a defensive campaign, employees are left to draw their own conclusions.

CHAPTER 11

Internal Communication

The house journal is an important tool of public relations. Almost all leading companies bring out house journals to communicate with their employees, shareholders, suppliers, dealers, etc. Companies hope to project a better image through house journals. As such, it is very important that the public relations personnel consider production of house journals a key task. Only a dedicated effort and total involvement will result in quality production of house journals.

In this study, the various steps to be considered before launching a house journal and the contents that are normally found in any house journal are discussed in depth. The element of care required in the production are also detailed, as well as major, if not all, aspects of printing and production of house journals. Today, the house journal is often communicated to employees by using the Internet or in house Intranet.

What is a house journal?

The house journal is a major medium of communication used by business and non-profit organizations in communication with employees, shareholders, suppliers, dealers, customers, and the general public.

Objectives of a house journal

House journals periodically carry the image and message of the organization to specific publics. A house journal is produced mainly to:

▶ Inform

▶ Interpret

▶ Motivate

▶ Educate

▶ Entertain

▶ Build team spirit

▶ Persuade

▶ Get feedback

The purpose is to improve the morale of the employees, create a favorable climate for the working of the organization, and promote and provide opportunities for creative expression.

TYPES OF HOUSE JOURNALS

The three principal types of house journals are:

▶ **Internal:** Published for employees of a company, business, or professional association or members of a non-profit organization

▶ **External:** Published for the general public, opinion leaders, suppliers, dealers, and shareholders

▶ **Combination:** Published for both internal and external publics

Basic principles and factors involved

▶ **Decide why a house journal.** When the organization grows in major dimensions by assets, labor force, product range, administration, marketing, and sales it becomes necessary to minimize the gap of communication and feedback of information. The only available and economic means is the house journal publication, by which the workers, shareholders, consumers, dealers, sales force, etc., are kept informed of events worth their attention. Minimizing communication gaffs is important from all points of view, and especially toward company harmony, thereby a rise in productivity, the ultimate aim being the profitability of the organization concerned.

▶ **Study company publication background**

▶ **Set company policies.** Decide at the outset whether the company is the type of organization which, by virtue of its history, present activities, and future plans, can benefit by issuing a publication. Some worthy, well-managed companies in the past started publications that were discontinued, in spite of adequate presentation, because internal conditions of various kinds were unfavorable to their success. On the other hand, there are many organizations in which a well planned periodical would knit together a lot of loose ends and prove an invaluable instrument for the promotion of essential internal or external policies.

▶ **Define aims and purposes.** Determine definitely what the company wishes to accomplish by starting a publication. Decide upon the objectives and shape the program to achieve them. Don't start a publication in a spirit of imitation simply because the competitors issue papers which are highly commended.

▶ **Formulate publishing policies.** Having determined the objectives, set a definite but not too rigid policy for attaining them. This requires decisions on fundamental problems. If an internal journal is considered, the policies must be shaped to accomplish some or all of many purposes. Some of these major objective are:

▶ To build up an esprit de corps; to make the working force, insofar as possible, contented with their jobs and surroundings and willing to give their loyalty and support because they feel that the organization is the right place to work.

▶ To increase production by publicizing incentives, by inspiring friendly competition, publishing and rewarding suggestions, explaining the urgency and advantage of greater production and reduced costs, or by any other ethical means.

▶ To quiet labor unrest. The procedures adapted to this purpose are too involved for discussion purposes here, but it is important to let employees know their importance to the company and that the future and security they may enjoy is a reward for satisfactory service.

▶ To provide the working force with information about the company, its background, history, past accomplishments, products, plans, and projects, outside reputation, problems and, in particular, its financial status and operations.

▶ To contribute to the education of workers by well-selected articles on such subjects as history, economics, current events, world affairs, science and inventions, human progress, etc., as well as providing practical help for everyday living so well presented in special sections. Other projects which merit careful consideration are the promotion of health and recreation, social activities, savings, cooperatives, and community cooperation.

▶ **Planning the external publication.** If an external journal is considered, the policy decisions are much less complicated than in the case of the internal. The external is primarily intended to promote business by increasing sales or expanding distribution. A properly edited external publication, because of its elasticity, regularity, and readability, can contribute to business promotion with many approaches that could not be made, even at much greater cost, by the ordinary methods of direct mail or even by trade publications or general advertising.

The primary policy questions to be decided by a company planning an external journal are:

▶ **How many sales customers or prospect groups should be covered in the journal's circulation?** This decision is predicated on cost, inside conditions and problems, and general objectives. In many cases, externals, and often internals as well, are distributed to directors, company bankers, community leaders, shareholders, and others who may have a direct interest in the finances and general progress of the business. There are many obvious advantages in such distribution.

▶ **Should it be placed on product or service selling?** In other words, should the journal be used mainly as a vehicle to offer present available products or to announce other products or services soon to be available? Most publishers prefer a happy medium that promotes both institutional prestige and immediate or future business.

Reporters and correspondents

Correspondents are usually employees representing the editor in various departments of the company. If the editor permits his correspondents to run to extremes with petty personal items, his or her publication soon will degenerate into gossip, which is the target for criticism from many who wish sincerely to see the company paper assume its rightful place as a dignified and purposeful instrument of useful information..

On the other hand, it must be remembered that reporters and correspondents work, for the most part, without compensation. Almost everyone enjoys seeing his or her name or picture in the paper. If the editor kills too many items, the correspondents lose interest in their work and the editor has a serious turnover problem to add to the editor's difficulties.

FORMAT OF THE HOUSE JOURNAL

The selection of format must be based on various considerations, including economy, frequency, size of pictures, quantity, method of distribution, objectives, etc. House publications fall into three broad classifications:

▶ The bulletin or newsletter

▶ The tabloid newspaper

▶ The magazine

The Bulletin, which is a digest of news for busy readers, is often referred to as the "lowliest of the low," but its value cannot be underestimated. It has a definite niche in the field; it has the advantage of speedy and economical reproduction; it is more personal than its more expensive brothers.

The Tabloid Newspaper is difficult to publish. A weakness of the newspaper house publication is emulation of the daily paper in everything but size. Several things wrong with the average newspaper, which also apply to the newspaper type house publication, are: copy too long, type too small, columns too narrow, and headlines too involved.

The Magazine provides the greatest variation in size and proportion of all house publications. The magazine style company publication should be standardized at three sizes:

▶ The *Reader's Digest* size for those composed entirely of copy

▶ The weekly size for those composed chiefly of illustrations

▶ The 8.5" × 11" or trade journal size, for those that are a little of both

The last-listed size is still the popular one, both for internals and externals in the magazine style.

FREQUENCY AND LANGUAGE

There should not be too large a gap between issues, otherwise the sense of regularity and continuity will be lost. Readers should look forward to the next issue, and it should appear on a regular day, such as the first of the month. Frequency may be determined by the need to publish news as soon as possible or the greater timeliness of feature articles. Normal frequency is once every three months. The language of the house journal is preferably English as well as any other predominant local languages of the majority of workers/ employees. Or in many organizations, bilingual journals are published and, where budget allows, one is published in English and others are published in different languages.

BUDGET ALLOCATION

The allocation of funds for the purpose of a house journal is an investment in disguise. The following are the elements of this budget.

▶ Frequency or periodicity of the journal

▶ Format of the journal

▶ Size of the journal

▶ Number of pages in each issue

▶ Process of printing

▶ Illustrations, photographs, etc.

▶ Black and white or color

▶ Blank/designs

▶ Quality of paper

▶ Salaries/wages

▶ Distribution

▶ Mailing cost

▶ Circulation cost

▶ Administrative expenses

INFORMATION AND FEEDBACK

The editor of the house journal will require different types of news materials for each issue including feature articles, photographs, etc., from various departments of the organization concerned. Each head of department is to be briefed to send suitable material before a certain designated date to insert in a particular issue.

Freelance photographers should be engaged to attend the various functions, meetings, conferences, events of importance, visits of VIPs, etc.

A house journal will be attractive only if the photographs and feature stories of interest to the readers and their families are published in it. Persons working in the organization who have an interest in reading and writing should be invited to contribute interesting material. Use of the internet will permit inclusion of video clips, animation, and other features such as PowerPoint slide presentations.

CHAPTER 12

Corporate Image

Whatever the perspective, image advertising, when properly executed, can help dramatically to move the corporation toward meeting corporate goals. It is, in fact, the very leading edge of corporate strategy, essential in positioning a company for maximum growth.

In terms of customer relations, image advertising deals with perceptions. We have all heard the saying, "The customer is always right." But with corporate image, it isn't strictly whether the customer is right or wrong that matters. It's what he or she thinks about you that counts. Thus, every company, even the smallest, has an image, whether planned or not.

PERCEPTION IS REALITY

Corporate image begins with the public's perception of a company — the preconceived ideas and prejudices that have formed in the minds of customers. This perception may not always reflect accurately a corporation's true profile, but to the public it is reality. It is up to the CEO especially to be sure those initial impressions are molded into a positive force that will enhance business prospects for the corporation, or that they are sufficiently changed to match the actuality of the situation.

A BURGEONING BUSINESS

Although the major portion of a budget still goes into brand or product promotion, corporate image advertising expenditures are growing.

Why this tremendous and rapid growth? One reason is the soaring number of mergers, acquisitions, divestitures, and takeovers, which continue to change the corporate scene drastically. They alter both the realities of the companies involved and the perceptions of those companies held by their various publics. Added to this confusion on the corporate scene are the deregulation of banks and other financial institutions and the invasion of international advertisers into the media.

In times of financial turmoil, customers, shareholders, employees, and others begin to wonder about a company's products, profits, directions, and future. Clearly, they need to be told what has happened, what is happening, and what is going to happen. A corporation undergoing important changes needs to present its new reality to its public and needs to create a new environment for up-to-date perceptions.

THE MISSION OF IMAGE ADVERTISING

Although experts may disagree as to the exact number, there are at least seven basic missions for image advertising. Properly conceived and implemented, image advertising can be the leading edge of corporate strategy for your company, helping to:

▶ build public awareness and acceptance and establish a more favorable market position.

▶ redefine your corporation after a merger, takeover, acquisition, or name change.

▶ pre-sell target markets to support product marketing.

▶ influence shareholders and the financial community.

▶ establish your company's position on timely issues.

▶ assist in the management of a crisis situation.

▶ attract and hold quality employees, while creating a cooperative environment in their communities.

Whatever the mission, an image campaign should be market driven and should have specific objectives. Those objectives may often apply to more than one mission. In other words, a campaign to announce a name change can do much more than merely make an announcement. It can also make the general public more aware of the corporation and its strengths, generate interest in company brands, pass along important information to the financial community, and influence potential employees

THREE BASIC INGREDIENTS FOR SUCCESS

What makes for successful image advertising? Whatever the mission, three factors are almost always involved:

DIRECTION OR FOCUS

Have you done the necessary research to articulate your corporate mission . . . to set the right goals? . . . to know the audience(s) you must influence? . . . to select the media to best reach your target publics?

CREATIVITY

Will your advertising really "cut through the clutter? . . . be noticed? . . . be remembered? . . . be acted upon?

CONSISTENCY

Will your campaign run long enough to have real value? Will all your advertising carry the same theme, support the same message, even abroad?

Other factors, of course, may seem equally important in given situations. Even so, these three basic ingredients, properly implemented, are a sure recipe for a workable image campaign that gets results. In the remainder of this chapter we will examine them each in turn.

Establish your direction or focus

In image advertising, it's the responsibility of the CEO to determine the campaign's mission, or missions, what new image is required, and later judge whether set goals are being met.

David Ogilvy, who has been responsible for more successful corporate campaigns than anyone can probably remember, said in reference to a campaign created by his agency for IBM:

> *Every commercial and every advertisement we did had to be submitted to Tom Watson and his brother, Dick, at the top. It was all done at the top level. I think that's just as it should be. It is a waste of money for any corporation to do corporate advertising unless they define the purpose of that advertising. In my judgment . . . it should be defined by the head of your corporation — for three reasons:*

➤ If you get the top individuals to define the purpose, they're more likely to keep the campaign going. Corporate campaigns which don't have the personal involvement of the chief executive don't last long.

➤ The top person in your company is the only one who is in a position to reconcile the conflicting purposes of the different departments in the company.

➤ Only the top person in a company can find enough money to do the job.

Part of the job description of the top person in any corporation should be to define the corporation's purpose, and to define it in such a way that will be relevant far into the future. In this manner, corporate advertising — unlike brand advertising — becomes the voice of the chief executive and his or her board of directors.

Whether or not the CEO actually initiates the corporate campaign, it is the CEO who is held responsible by the board and shareholders for its ultimate success or failure. Thus, an involved CEO will give the program active guidance and a strong sense of direction. The CEO must know and define, at least in some general sense, what specific problem needs to be solved and how the solution is to be developed. Focus is crucial because an image campaign can have significant impact on more than one area of the company. The primary objective should be an extension of long-term corporate strategy directed at those aspects of the business that hinder the company from fully achieving corporate goals.

Choose your target carefully

The target market for image advertising is known as the "corporate audience." It consists of those people who are capable of assimilating a corporate message and who are willing to consider more than one position before making up their minds on an issue or problem. They generally fall into four groups: business leaders, activists and opinion leaders, the financial community, and government leaders.

Customers and prospects, employees and potential employees, investors, and the trade are also prime targets for many advertisers. Don't overlook the media itself. It's important that their perceptions of your company correspond with the corporate image you wish to promote. This is doubly true if you are involved with the management of some crisis situation.

The selection of just the right audience — or combination of audiences — depends upon strategy and mission. Whatever your goal, image advertising gives your company an unmatched opportunity to present a particular point of view, exactly as you wish to communicate it, to precisely the right people.

Creativity and consistency

The great problem with corporate advertising — as with product advertising — is that so much of it is done so badly. And if the ads aren't any good, nothing much may happen. Most people, even many in the advertising business, don't really know the difference between good advertising and bad. They don't understanding why one ad might sell 10 or 15 times as much as another for the same product. There is a very real difference.

There are those advertisers that fail to define the purpose of their corporate advertising, or they may assign too many purposes to it. Or they may not identify their target audience accurately or completely. Very often, too, they make the mistake of not measuring results. They fly blind. How then can they possibly know for sure how effective their corporate advertising is?

There is, of course, no formula for creative excellence. But there are certain guidelines to follow, certain pitfalls to beware of. David Ogilvy puts it this way:

> *Corporation advertising should not insult the intelligence of the public. It should be plainspoken, candid, adult, honest, intelligent, and specific. It should avoid parchment or self-congratulation. It should be rooted in products or capabilities or services or policies. It should be interesting . . . you cannot bore people into admiring your company.*

> *Corporate advertising requires creative genius to penetrate the indifference with which people regard most corporations. If nobody reads the message except you, nothing is going to happen. You can't save souls in an empty church.*

FORMS, THEMES, MEDIA

Successful image advertising comes in many styles and shapes — long editorial copy or short sales copy; photography, illustration, or all type; inserts, spreads, single pages, and even fractional units; color or black and white — in just about every combination possible, and in a bewildering assortment of business, trade, and consumer magazines and newspapers. And don't forget the electronic media and the internet.

Some campaigns feature products or service. Some talk about capabilities or markets served. Still others establish corporate philosophy. Whatever the format, whatever the theme, whatever the media, each image campaign featured in this book was carefully, even lovingly, conceived and executed. All have been successful in their own way; and while some may seem more "creative" than others — beauty is in the eye of the beholder — all worked, and there's a lesson to be learned from each.

Although there is no formula that guarantees great ads, there are three questions, the answers to which can lead to good corporate as well as good product advertising.

"The *first* question is **Who? Who are you talking to?** Demand a detailed description of the target audience. The better you know your customers, the better you can sell them.

"The *second* question is **What? What do you say to them?** You're looking for that one salient appeal. . . . Only the **Who?** people know for sure, so ask them. Good research leads to good advertising.

"Answering the *third* question first is the single biggest reason for third-rate advertising. The question is **How? How do you say it?** Execution makes or breaks advertising. It can break it if you haven't answered the first two questions before [the third].

"These three questions should lead to good advertising, which is defined as the right execution of the right appeal to the right audience."

Six guides to success

We have seen that all corporate image advertising is not alike. Different companies have different problems, different needs, and perceive the marketplace — and the world — through different eyes.

In the creation and preparation of almost every successful image campaign, however, certain basic guides are generally followed. These are:

▶ **Perception** is what counts. It's not necessarily the reality of a situation but what your target audience believes to be reality that creates corporate image.

▶ **Direction** for an image campaign should be established at the top, usually by the CEO. He or she is the only one who understands the company from all viewpoints, can employ personal involvement toward reconciling conflicts between divisions and departments, can keep the campaign going on track, and can find the necessary budget to get the job done.

▶ **Know thyself.** You've got to know who you are before you can decide where you're going. What is your image? Do you need an image campaign at all? Some companies don't, of course. In other words, employ research — before, during, and after any image program.

▶ **Focus.** Do you know who you are trying to reach? The better you understand your audience(s), the better you can influence their perceptions of your company.

▶ **Creativity.** What will your campaign say to its target publics? What single specific appeal will best "cut through the clutter" to be remembered and acted upon? Study your audience; they are the only ones who can provide the answer.

▶ **Consistency.** It goes hand-in-hand with creativity. The execution of your advertising — or the how of it — must be dependent upon the answers to who and what. By nature, it must involve not only consistency of theme but also of exposure, or your entire investment may be wasted.

A company's image is a composite of all its actions, including communications. How a company communicates is very much a part of what it does. All internal and external communications produced for a company contribute to its image by both demonstrating and advocating.

The concept of "corporate advertising" focuses on the subject of image too narrowly. Since all communications are seen as contributing to the corporate image, no one method or audience is more or less important than the others.

Chapter 13

Digital Age of Public Relations

The new media has a powerful arsenal of tools that can help an organization manage its image and reputation and improve its sales by going directly to its stakeholders. This option to by pass the traditional media creates new ways to make organizational messages heard in the U.S. and around the world. This approach also gives public relations and marketing executives new opportunities to plan PR campaigns with "buzz", and it has feedback mechanisms for telling organizations what their customers really think about a company's products and services.

So why participate in cyberspace? Is this just a fad that will go away in time? No. The Internet is here to stay and it can help an organization engage in new conversations with target publics that are unavailable with traditional media. With these new conversations on the net and feedback from customers and stakeholders, organizations will be able to launch new products, improve old products, and reach out to new and younger audiences. Cyberspace is like the "Old West" where prospectors searched for gold and new business opportunities. By joining the cyberspace community, a company can learn that customers and stakeholders want an interactive relationship and that they are willing to help an organization find new opportunities for partnering with them.

The new media is not just about finding new opportunities, although that it an important component. It is about building effective on- line communication programs that can help drive website traffic. New on-line customers can be a totally different breed from the brick and mortar customers that organizations have come to rely on for the past decade. The digital age is a brave new world that can become a catalyst for organizations to try new experiments, try new pilot programs on the net, reach out to new markets, and try new forms of communications.

On-line communications should also help an organization build its reputation with cyberspace influentials and luminaries, the new cyber journalists and bloggers who are changing the landscape in how public relations and marketing are practiced in the digital age. A website that has positive press from journalists and bloggers can distinguish an organization apart from its competitors. A-list influencers on line, including top bloggers in your field can and often do sway public opinion. B-list bloggers can post information about an organization that enhances its reputation; however, they can also post negative information that can hurt sales of products and shine a poor light on management.

The public relations team needs to monitor bloggers' comments on the web. Given what is know about the blogosphere today, managing a company's reputation on-line may be one of the most important tasks of 21st century organizations. It is imperative that organizations build a strong presence on the web to offset any negative comments or misperceptions about an organization.

Another organizational benefit from having effective on-line communications is the ability for public relations and marketing executives to share ideas and collaborate with customers and stakeholders. This is simply a matter of conducting better conversations and receiving better feedback from people who matter to the organization and its management. Think of the benefit of receiving just one big idea or insight from these on-line conversations with customers and stakeholders, enabling an organization to chart a new course and expand its business.

Researchers in public relations and marketing have suggested that the Internet has provided a new outlet for capturing specialized knowledge and insights for improving communications between the organization and its publics. Typically, organizations have offered a one way communication model: We talk. You listen. On-line communications is more receptive to two-way communications and collaboration. We talk. We also listen. Interactivity on-line is the bridge to better communications because it takes into consideration another viewpoint that can and often differ from the prevailing wisdom of management. After all, discovering what others really think about your organization is becoming more vital as the Internet plays an increasingly significant role in everyone's lives.

Public relations and marketing executives are hiring vendors to monitor what is being said about their organizations on the web. A rumor about a product's performance, a discussion about a pending merger can translate into positive or negative public relations. New digital tools can help the public relations and marketing executives mange the cyberspace landscape with self-confidence and success.

NEW DIGITAL TOOLS

This list details how the following digital tools can help an organization communicate more effectively in cyberspace.

Blogs

A blog is a website by an individual or organization that posts information (opinion) on the Internet for others' comment and reactions. Blogging is now one of the fastest growing ways in which individuals and organizations can be heard in the blogosphere. The freedom to express one's ideas is a blogger's dream. Bloggers can experiment with new ways to promote and share their ideas on the Internet with others, who are often similarly-minded.

Public relations professionals are beginning to appreciate the power of blogging for their organizations. For a relatively inexpensive investment, a new blogger can be on the Internet in less than a week discussing important issues or recent development about a company's research and development activities, or its new products or services.

This opportunity to go directly to the buyer or stakeholder can be more authentic than direct marketing and provide an outlet for feedback from other like-minded bloggers in one's field. Blogging can accomplish three goals for an organization. First, it can build a niche voice for products, service, or major ideas. For example, politicians use blogs to reach voters across the country and companies can blog brand-new information about themselves to customers daily or even hourly. Second, blogging can help an organization share conversations about what is occurring in its industry. An organization can pioneer or trailblaze new technology or new services in a given field. Third, blogging can create a feedback mechanism for buyers and stakeholders to tell the organization what they think and provide the management team with helpful advice on ways to move ahead for the future.

Public relations professionals now recognize that bloggers have changed and will continue to change the way an organization conducts its business. The CBS network was apparently caught off guard when bloggers charged that the CBS news staff was airing on national television an apparently forged letter about George Bush's military service in the Air National Guard. Some persons at CBS were discharged because of the controversy. Bloggers have challenged Intel and other major corporations on product flaws, eventually leading to major recalls. Corporations such as McDonalds and Wal-Mart are using blogs to build their reputation and create campaigns on the web.

Podcasting

Podcasting is a personal broadcast on the Internet in digital audio or video format which is available on line for downloading to a personal computer, iPod, iPhone, or MP3 player. A podcast is similar to being on the radio or TV without being restricted to a specific time slot. Podcasting can effectively distribute an organization's key messages to customers and stakeholders with some moderate help from the information technology (IT).

Podcasts are relatively easy to create and allow visitors to enter your website and learn about products and services, executive presentations, speeches and marketing programs. As a very important tool for public relations and marketing professionals, podcasts have significant benefits. The human voice, for example, is a powerful persuasive instrument for listeners saturated with mechanical voices in a digital world. Most people prefer hearing a real voice on topics of personal importance. Thus, the auditory or video component connected to the podcast can be very influential in a public relations or marketing campaign.

Moreover, with a podcast, organizations are not limited to reaching customers in only one geographical region. Like-minded customers from around the world can download a podcast and listen or see it later at their convenience. While podcasting is somewhat more complicated to set up than a blog, a public relations team can still be up and running in less than a week with an initial investment in equipment (microphone, software and website) installed by your IT department or vendor. Podcasting and blogging can be integrated in what is called V-Logging.

In a public relations campaign for your organization, CEO speeches, marketing pitches, and commentary about the organization can be broadcast over the Internet using a podcast. Even though this is relatively new technology compared to old media, the power to share an organization's viewpoint in a non-text format can position the organization ahead of competitors. **RSS** is a feed via the Internet that allows a podcast to be transmitted with a tag to customers or stakeholders who have an interest in your organization's ideas, products and services. RSS syndication helps customers find a particular podcast, subscribe to it, and download it to their computer or other device.

Wikis

Wiki is a website that anyone can update, delete, or edit information. For example, Wikipedia is the free encyclopedia that has challenged the Britannica Encyclopedia franchise in the world of information. With wikis, anyone can express opinions on line, in chat rooms, on message boards and on forums. Many organizations are using wikis for knowledge management, project follow-up and training employees.

With blogs, podcasting and wikis, organizations can position themselves as digital-friendly and open for business in the blogosphere. As noted, the key element in these new digital tools is interactivity. While traditional media can deliver the same message, it is more difficult to obtain direct feedback. By using blogs, podcasts, and wikis to manage cyberspace communications, organizations are demonstrating to their customers and stakeholders that their opinion matters; at the same time these are excellent tools for directing information to important target publics in selected markets.

The era of one way conversations between the organization and its publics is disappearing and being replaced with two-way communications that give customers open access to the organization in real time on the web. The office no longer ends its business day at 6:00pm. Cyberspace is a 24/7 operation on the web. Before these tools were available to public relations and marketing executives, many important contributions from customers and stakeholders were no doubt lost because of limited access to the organization.

Social Media

Social media is often associated with web sites that allow people to exchange information, network, and invite friends to be part of their life on the web. Finding ideas for new products and learning what young people are saying to each other is worth a visit to social networking sites such as MySpace and Facebook, two of the most popular social networking sites on the Web. More people are turning to these sites for conversation, advice, meeting friends, and planning for the future.

Public relations and marketing directors need to learn more about social networking and how it can help their organization in shaping its marketing and public relations programs. These sites are valuable sources to spot new trends and learn more about your future customers and stakeholders. However, one disturbing finding from researchers is that more young people are abandoning traditional media such as print newspapers and relying more on the Internet and social networking sites for news and other types of information. Keeping that sober reality in mind, public relations managers should consider reaching social networking sites in their public relations plan. This approach can be used as a way to position their organization with the next generation of customers.

Although Facebook and MySpace are aimed primarily at young people, professionals and business executives are turning to professional networking sites such as Linkedin as a way to network and build business relationships on the web. If you are a professional manager in public relations and marketing, you may be asked to create a profile on a social networking site to talk about your work and your range of professional activities. Experts in specialized fields such as photographers and media placement experts are signing up with Squidon so that colleagues can learn via the net what they are doing and become informed about their professional organizations and affiliations.

Viral Video

YouTube has been called the video outlet to the world. Owners of I-Phones and aficionados of the web often turn to YouTube for the latest, most popular downloaded videos posted on the Internet. YouTube gives anyone with a camera and an interesting topic a means to display a video for a global audience. Placing one's best video on YouTube almost guarantees an audience greater than a placement on NBC, CBS, and ABC combined.

A picture is worth a thousand words. To reach the video generation that grew up with computers, video games, and HDTV, it would be smart for an organization to produce a video for the massive YouTube audience as part of its public relations programming. The video, however, must be entertaining and authentic—not just a promo piece for an ad/pr campaign. A viral video on YouTube should be a pictoral account (usually about 3 minutes or less) about people, items, events, activities or other interesting trends about what is happening in world. The famous Ford modeling agency models has a recent hit on YouTube that garnered as many as a million viewers to the site. The models talked about photo shoots, fashion, and their workouts. This viral video approach to public relations using YouTube as a platform for publicity is further evidence that on-line communications can be incredibly effective for spreading the messages about any organization as well as its people, products and services.

After all, if a modeling agency and its models- or even less famous people can be a hit on YouTube, consider how on line video opportunities for the entertainment, technology, sports, and industrial segments of the economy can make their case with innovative publicity. Many consumers want to learn more about fashion, business, entertainment as well as other subjects they do not even realize would be of interest. These viewers who search for new and different videos are constantly seeking information about viral videos on

YouTube and assorted Internet sites-- and an effectively posted viral video will definitely draw their attention. One additional advantage of viral video is that it can be produced with music, comedy, and emotional buy-in to convey an important message and leave a lasting impression. Viral videos, I-Phones, I-Pods, MP3 players, and advanced cell phones have revolutionized the way images and pictures are seen and sent around the world.

Virtual Reality

Virtual reality was once considered the domain of science fiction novels and movies such as the Matrix. Experiments in peer to peer media are now occurring in cyberspace. A relatively new community on the web called Second Life actually has its own residents and currency. One can find Fortune 500 companies, media companies, real estate companies and other entrepreneurial organizations doing business in Second Life. Residents in this community can pick their own avatar identity and market their product and services to other residents.

Some analysts estimate that Second Life has over one million residents and that number keeps growing every month. From a public relations perspective, this is the next step in peer to peer media in a virtual world. Additionally, it is clearly an interesting place to meet customers, attract new media, and stay focused on a new trend.

It is also a radically different and crucial forum on which to experiment with new ideas, pilot new products, and promote an organizations presence on line in full dimension. As more potential customers and businesses join Second Life, it will not be surprising to find public relations practitioners holding press conferences and other events in a virtual community.

The inevitable new direction of digital public relations puts blogs, podcasting, wikis, social media, viral video, and virtual reality at the new frontier of communications. The new media impact on every aspect on modern life will shape the way society communicates in the 21st century.

Acknowledgements

This book has benefited from the advice and encouragement of many persons. The authors take full responsibility for what has been written and for any errors. Special thanks go to the support of the administration and faculty of both Iona College and TASMAC. We wish to thank Brooke Eads, Publishing Services Associate, and Molly Weddle, iUniverse Marketing Consultant, and other members of the staff at iUniverse for their assistance in the publication process. Special thanks go to Judie Szuets for her help in typing and editing the manuscript and the index of this book in several drafts. Finally, we wish to thank our families for all their support.

This book is dedicated to our families, as well as to public relations educators Dr. Otto Lerbinger and Dr. Bernard Rubin of Boston University and to the memory of public relations pioneers Raymond Wiley Miller of Harvard University and Edward L. Bernays of Boston University. This book is also dedicated to all who work or aspire to work in public relations.

Index

Printed in the United States
131261LV00006BA/3/P